# The Dream that inspired the Bible
A vision of hope for the whole creation

By Chris Sunderland

**EarthAbbey Publishing**

Published in 2009 by EarthAbbey Publishing, an initiative of Project Agora, charity registration number 1110788 and company number 4430518 registered in England and Wales at 50 Guest Avenue, Emersons Green, Bristol BS16 7GA

All profits from the sale of this book will go to the EarthAbbey fund within Project Agora

ISBN: 978-0-9561913-0-4

The book in your hands was printed on FSC (Forest Stewardship Council) Accredited paper. It is set in 11pt Georgia on a MacBook Pro using Adobe InDesign.

**they shall sit everyone under their vine and under their fig tree**

Micah 4

# Preface
## Why this book?

Human beings may be about to face the most serious trial of their existence. Our impact upon the earth can no longer be ignored. Whether it be cast in terms of climate change, peak oil, the extinction of creatures, the shortage of fresh water, or rising sea levels the message is clear: We have to live more in tune with the earth.

The last five years have seen an extraordinary shift in public consciousness. We are all now aware, to some degree, of the environmental issues that are bearing down upon us, but the strange thing is that the human response has so far been woefully inadequate. The reason for our failure to respond may be that we have not recognised that there is an essential spiritual dimension to these problems. There is clearly no lack of campaigns. Carbon reduction programmes and awareness-raising initiatives are everywhere, but these will not work unless we also address the deeper spiritual issues that are at stake. I think there are three dimensions to the spiritual challenge that we face as human beings.

The first concerns how we understand ourselves as human beings and our relationship to the earth. Our worldview affects not only the way we think, but also the way we live. We have grown used to telling our history as if we are the supreme actors and the earth is our stage. We can no longer do this. The earth cannot be viewed as simply there for our use. Instead we must know ourselves to be part of the web of life, acutely dependent on the intricate and complex eco-systems in which we are enmeshed. Such a radical change of perspective is hard to achieve. This should properly be conceived as a spiritual task.

The second spiritual dimension has to do with our wills. For centuries now, our so-called 'developed' society has encouraged people to pay prime attention to self-interest. The economic model that we have embraced teaches us that all good things flow from attention to self-interest. We are taught that wealth will come for all people if only we pay attention to a vision of economic growth that is at its heart corrupt, not only because it implies that the earth is an infinite resource, but also because it encourages human beings on a path of immediate self-gratification. Such a vision has been justified by a new generation of moralists who persuade us to see ourselves as consumers and self-gratification as our right and our freedom. The result of all this is that the 'developed' world has lost contact with the moral virtue of restraint, just at a time when we desperately need to place limits around our activities. This is a spiritual issue. There is a need for a change of heart and a reconstruction of the will.

Simple restraint is not a popular message in any human community unless it is tied to some vision of what can be attained through it. That is what happens in a war for instance. The great story of survival against an enemy becomes a means of uniting the people and encouraging sacrificial behaviour in any number of areas of life. This leads us to the third spiritual dimension of our problems today, which is to find a story that will give us hope for the future. Creating this story will be a primary task of the twenty first century. But where will it come from?

One of the functions of religion may be to help develop the story that unites. Yet the mainline faiths have not, in my opinion, been inspiring so far in their contribution to environmental issues. I have been a Christian now for more than thirty years, much of that time in leadership of some sort or another, and I confess that we have not adequately addressed the spiritual issues that I have identified above. Much of the time we have preached a version of the gospel that is basically about human beings, with a bit of creation thrown in at harvest time. Much of the time we have evaded gospel challenges about materialism and made excuses for our avaricious culture. And much of the time we have encouraged people toward sacrifice and restraint only around a very narrow band of sexual and sanctity of human life issues.

Unfortunately, there has also been a tendency for church people and environmentalists to develop a form of trench warfare, shooting each other down on the basis of the old, and partly misconceived, story of the relationship between Christianity and paganism. Christians are fearful of compromising their faith and being contaminated in some way by 'new age' beliefs, while many environmentalists have a deep aversion to anything 'religious', dismissing it as inherently oppressive and anti-earth. It seems to me that the only proper response to this antagonism is to plead for some discernment from both sides. Sure, there is religion that is oppressive, but there is also much that is not, and the history of religion is at least mixed. There have been some remarkable fruits of faith evident in human history. Likewise, there is a huge diversity of people engaged with the environmental movement today, some avowed atheists, many others with a whole range of creative and open approaches to spirituality. So let's be a bit subtle in our thinking and leave aside the simplistic defences.

Such discernment is particularly necessary when approaching religious texts. This book is based on the Bible. As a Christian, the Bible remains for me the most reliable means to engage with the faith as it arose. To read the Judaeo-Christian scriptures is to cut behind the accretions and distractions of a two thousand year old tradition back to the original lives of those who believed and the cultures of which they were a part. It can still be hard to work out what is going on, and there is a huge and diverse set of texts, but, on any account, these are a truly remarkable record. I take the Bible very seriously as my primary source of faith, yet this does not mean that I am wed to a set of doctrinal positions and interpretations that can be cast as any form of fundamentalism. Those who suffer from fundamentalism feel the need to impose a type of uniformity on scripture that simply is not there. The result is that they ignore or radically reinterpret enormous tracts of material in the interests of doctrinal conformity. I would suggest that this is, in practice, to be a great deal less serious about the text than it warrants.

Since becoming aware of the environmental challenges that we face, I have focussed on exploring the relationship that the people and communities in the Bible had with the earth and how their faith informed this. Of course, I am not the first, nor will I be the last to do this. But what has impressed itself on me is that these people had a dream of living at peace with the earth. As chapter by chapter of this book unfolds I will attempt to unpack the elements of this dream for you . I have found it an inspiring process to put it all together. For me it acts as a way to understand the work of God in the world, not necessarily to replace the other stories that we are accustomed to, but at least to lie alongside these others. I believe this dream may be important in addressing the spiritual need of this age.

## My thanks...

It is sometimes hard to know where ideas come from. For the last ten years I have been deliberately seeking ways of reading the Bible so as to relate faith to the public life of our society. Bible Society have been a constant and valued companion during much of this time. Their partnership with the Northumbria community, known as 'The Telling Place', was very fruitful ground for me. In the last few years I have also been particularly indebted to people in the environmental movement in Bristol. The Transition movement has been inspiring. Vala Ragnarsdottir, Professor of Environmental Sustainability at Bristol University and her World Cafe team have led me and many others to dream new things. The practical realities of change have been learnt through *Chooseday*, a green travel initiative, that we have pioneered in Bristol and I owe a debt of gratitude to the many who have worked on this, often voluntarily. I am also aware of a seminar given by Tom and Christine Sine on Shalom as an educational model that sowed important seeds and an inspiring day with A Rocha that caused me to think afresh about the story of the Prodigal Son.

On a more practical note, I am grateful to Alan Mann for commenting on and correcting the manuscript. My thanks also to Bruce Stanley, a member of EarthAbbey's creative team, whose skilful hand has created the artwork of this book.

To the many unnamed others who have also helped me along the way, thank you.

## Chris Sunderland September 2008

# Chapter One
## Living in a Prophetic Age

We are living at a crucial moment in earth history. For the first time a species has arisen that is making a serious impact on the earth's own biological, geological and climatic systems. The seriousness of this is being expressed by geologists, who are proposing to call the current age the Anthropocene, meaning the age of the humans. Human beings are now so powerful through their technology, and so numerous and so irresponsible that we are changing the climate, melting the glaciers and extinguishing other species. Bill McKibben describes human influence on the planet as *The End of Nature*. For him, there is no longer any real wilderness, where nature is left to itself, but human beings have made their mark everywhere. Everest is a pile of litter. The Russians have planted a flag under the Arctic sea to claim its oil and gas reserves. The rainforests are diminishing by the minute. The tale goes on. Mary Colwell is a producer in the BBC Natural History Unit and is in touch with many wildlife researchers and presenters. She has summed up the crisis by saying that we are already in the midst of the sixth great extinction of species on the earth, and the difference this time is that it is coming about because of human beings.

I was recently asked to give a talk to eleven hundred students and staff at a secondary school about climate change and our need to respond. I pondered quite deeply about what I was to say. They knew the science. They didn't want to hear that again. I decided in the end to begin with an apology. I told them that I was born in the nineteen fifties and that my generation has been dubbed the Babyboomers, as part of the burst in population growth in the postwar period, but that we would actually become famous for something else. I explained that since my birth, human beings had used half the earth's supply of conventional oil. It is a truly terrible statistic. Oil has been laid down in the earth since the Jurassic period, approximately 200 million years ago. It is a phenomenally concentrated form of energy and so easy to use that we have simply burnt half of it up in fifty years and spewed the resulting carbon dioxide into the atmosphere. I apologised to these young people, because it is evident that their generation will suffer from profound energy insecurity because of our action, that their generation will have to deal with the fallout from climate change in terms of poverty, famine and political unrest and that their generation will see a massive loss of biodiversity. I wondered whether I had said too much, whether young people could really cope with this. I was heartily encouraged over the following days to see that these young people really did want to rise to the challenge.

Let's put some numbers on this so we can see it in all its starkness. In 1950 the world was using 10m barrels of oil per day. In 2008 that number has risen to 86m barrels of oil per day and the world demand for oil continues to increase at the rate of 2-3% per year as more and more countries industrialise. Despite much-hyped claims for new oil in the media, the truth is that most of the world's really big oil fields were discovered in the middle of the last century and are now in the second half of their life, when the oil comes harder and is both more difficult and more expensive to extract each year. As a result oil production from major oil fields is declining at the rate of about 5% per year. If demand continues to grow while production declines, it is not hard to see that there will be a crunch point where demand exceeds supply. Some people are saying that we either have reached, or are just about to reach, that point. The year 2008 has seen dramatically high oil prices followed by global recession on the back of a banking crisis. The recession has lowered oil demand and the price has fallen, but commentators are well aware that if the economy picks up, then the oil price is likely to go sky high again. Our oil-addicted culture is suddenly in a very difficult position.

Secondly, in 1950 the global atmospheric concentration of carbon dioxide was 310 parts per million (ppm), having risen from a pre-industrial base of 280ppm in the late 1700s. It is now running at 386ppm and we have set a target to prevent it rising above 450ppm by 2050. That target is looking like a tall order at this point and catastrophic climate change is a reasonable fear.

Finally, world population in 1950 was 2.5 billion. It has now risen to 6.7 billion people and is forecast to rise to around 9 or 10 billion by 2050. We have managed to feed the world through this massive growth period by developing high yield staple crops of wheat, rice and maize coupled with the application of huge quantities of fertiliser and pesticide. The problem is that much of this 'green revolution' has been dependent on oil and other fossil fuels, which are utilised in the production of fertiliser and pesticides and the powering of irrigation systems.

These three factors, the end of cheap oil, climate change and world population are inextricably linked to one another. For example, what can be more basic or important than feeding the world? Political leaders thought they saw an easy answer to oil scarcity and climate change through growing biofuels for transportation. The problem was that, in many cases, fields were taken out of use that would otherwise produce food. The US, for example, intends to turn around a third of their maize harvest over to ethanol production. Similar decisions across the world were part of what led to a scarcity of staple crops in 2008, a food price rise and food riots in over thirty countries. This is but the beginning of the struggles.

## Our need for a story

We cannot deny that human beings are very powerful. The big question is whether we have the imagination to recognise our impact on the earth and respond constructively. There has already been an extraordinary surge in public consciousness about climate change. There is much talk about 'targets' from our leaders, but it is mostly talk and as yet there is very little evidence of the truly radical action required. The real sticking point must be somewhere else. I suspect that we are actually dealing with a much more pervasive, spiritual disease that has to do with how we view ourselves as human beings and our relationship with the earth and its creatures. The problem in a nutshell is that we have lost the plot. We have no dream.

I grew up with the agonised lyrics of Freddie Mercury. 'Does anyone know just what we are living for', he cried. His deep angst resonated with so much in a culture which found that it could criticise the past but not give hope for the future. The same is true today. Many of us feel to be going through the motions of life, making our time as pleasant as possible, acting out our days, finding meaning in the little things, but with a sort of emptiness within somewhere, because we really have no big picture about life, no dream, no big hope.

The evidence for this is all around us. We have somehow corrupted the natural optimism of many of our young people. If young people today are asked about their dreams, many can only speak of fame. For them that is how you become real. Celebrities have become our role models. Their banal, empty and confused existences are paraded before us in our glossy magazines as the life to yearn for. This celebrity culture reached an horrific low point in 2007 when a spate of young people in Wales hung themselves and left internet messages which suggested that this might be a perverse attempt at becoming famous. What has become of us? When we are facing the greatest challenges that human society has ever known, when we simply must work together like never before, we find that our people sense that they have really nothing to live for, but the fame of killing themselves. This suggests a deep corruption of the human soul. The same type of meaninglessness is evident in the United States as well. There the word Columbine sends shudders down the spine. Wave after wave of school massacres have devastated the society as sick people try to create some significance for their lives. Of course these are extreme cases, but they are indicative of a wider discomfort.

The psychologist, Oliver James, has studied the evidence for emotional distress in the English speaking industrialised nations of the world and finds that an extraordinary 23% of people in countries like the UK and the USA show clinical signs of mental and emotional disorder[1]. Where has this come from? It is worth charting a little more deeply how we got to

1    Oliver James *The Selfish Capitalist* 2008

be where we are. Some of it has been planned and some of it has just happened.

Adam Curtis in his acclaimed television documentary, *The Century of the Self*, told the story of Edward Bernays. This man was a psychologist, actually a cousin of Sigmund Freud. He was living at the time of the end of the First World War and the authorities came to him with a question. They said, 'The war brought people together, but who will keep the peace?' In other words, what will people rally around now that war is over? Some recognised the serious possibility of social and economic collapse. Bernays responded with an idea which would link economic growth with human happiness. His first 'triumph' was with smoking. At the time women were not smoking. It was a man thing. Bernays realised that in psychological terms the cigarette was a sign of the male organ and it represented independence and strength. So this is what he did. He hired a group of female debutantes, rich girls in society, to join a great parade. At the same time he tipped off the press that something was going to happen. At a given sign all the girls hitched up their skirts to reveal a pack of cigarettes, which they then lit, while the press were fed the phrase 'Torches of freedom'. So it was that women took to smoking. Freedom and independence, two qualities that women desired, were associated with a product, the cigarette. The general idea was that when people are trying to sell things they should associate the product with people feeling better about themselves. That way the economy grows and people are kept happy. Bernays called it propaganda, a way of keeping people happy. Others persuaded him to use the more acceptable, and then novel, term 'public relations'.

I mention that story because I think it lies at the heart of our current disease. In the absence of any dream around which we can unite, we have embraced a false substitute, a way of getting happy, which is more like a drug than anything else. And it is currently destroying the earth. All the advertisers now use this approach. They all associate their product with something we want to feel about ourselves. Whether it is the 4×4 on the great estate, or the perfume associated with 'because you're worth it' the psychological technique is the same. We call it retail therapy. Oliver James has exposed this as false comfort. The materialist hopes of our generation only satisfy for a moment, but soon leave us needing another fix and in a worse mental condition than before.

There was something very confident about the earlier part of the twentieth century. Science was going to change the world and make it better for all. The economic system was going to make everybody prosperous in the end. Human ingenuity had no limits - and neither did the earth. This utopian vision took no account of natural resources or our tendency to pollute. It had little to say about ourselves as creatures and participants in a great interconnecting living system of life. And it had little to say about God as creator, which was an idea that had become altogether rather embarrassing in the light of the battle between science and fundamentalists.

The thing that challenged this, at least for this part of the globe, were the two world wars. People were treated in such a terrible way. The language of science was used to justify hideous actions, like exterminating the Jews. There was the shocking power of the bombs unleashed on Hiroshima and Nagasaki and the dawning realisation that human beings might actually wipe each other out. The society that grew through these things had to ask radical questions about itself and its set of justifying stories. Ultimately, in the '70s and '80s a new generation was born, which has been dubbed 'post-modern', which would cast a sceptical eye over the whole society. To someone like the philosopher, Jean-Francois Lyotard, all institutions were suspect. We should question the great justifying myths that keep up the social order. They can all too easily lead us astray. For example, those alive in the '60s might remember 'Dixon of Dock Green' and its simple presentation of the police as upholders of social order. You would not get a show like that today. Instead the prevailing consensus is that we need reality shows, with cameras and insults and corrupt, but 'real' police. Similarly you can no longer have 'Tomorrow's World', another '60s TV product, with its easy parade of discoveries that are going to make life so much better. Instead you must realise that science can produce horror. The postmodern view is that scepticism is safe while big justifying myths are dangerous and always loaded with hidden and unexplored assumptions.

There was something right and helpful about all this. It certainly provided a much needed questioning about where we were. The problem is that it had nothing constructive to say. It merely created a vacuum in society. And into that vacuum, as we have seen, strode the marketplace, the purported saviour of society[2]. If there was nothing we could say about how we should live then we need a sop, something to keep us happy, and that is shopping.

## The end of political dreams and the right to party on the earth

A very similar corruption has taken place at the political level. Many governments today do not quite govern. Those that have bought into the 'neoliberal' economic model feel their primary and nonnegotiable task is to ensure a continual increase in Gross Domestic Product. This economic mandate is 'the elephant in the room' of all discussions of environmental policy. It is the reason, for example, why the government

........................................................

2      Bauman Z *Intimations of Postmodernity* Routledge 1992

of the UK waxes lyrical about tough carbon reductions while overseeing massive airport expansion. 'It is the economy stupid', as the phrase goes. The neo-liberal economic model functions as a form of fundamentalism distinguished by its refusal to listen to either science or faith. It has, for example, to shut its ears to climate change science when that science threatens economic growth. At the same time it fails to react to the now very evident failure of market growth to make for human well-being.

Matthew Taylor served as Chief Advisor on political strategy to Tony Blair's government a few years ago. In an interview on *The World this Weekend* in 2007, he confessed his belief that our current political system is in its death throes. He said that the parties have lost their identity and now all compete on the same ground. Reduced to a 'what works' mental-ity, they have nothing around which to build and are soon to fade away. This is shocking stuff from one who has spent most of his life immersed in political ideology and practice. But it became even more interesting when he was pressed to say what would happen in the future. Taylor replied that the politics of the future would belong to those who can talk the language of sustainability, and he meant by this not only the environment, but also a new vision of relationships and com-munity life. It was like he was saying that a whole new story was arising in the world.

Others have spotted the same problem. Jonathan Porritt says,

*"These days, it seems that just about every politician on earth is having a bit of a problem with 'the vision thing'. So few of the old ideas any longer seem capable of delivering*

*the goods; so many of the 'new' ideas look remarkably like the old ones recycled!"*[3]

Other changes in society have not been planned so much as just happened, like cars and aeroplanes for instance. One important contributor to the weakening of local community life and the rise of individualism in general is the availability of cheap, high-speed transport. We now feel free to travel where we like when we like. Families locate themselves all over the world aware that their loved ones are just a short car or aeroplane trip away. People think nothing of commuting thirty or forty miles to work. One person travels across Europe to see a dentist, while another lives in Glasgow and works in London. It has been easy, too easy. We have played upon the earth in truly reckless style. Future generations will treat transport as precious. Oil will not be easily replaced. Yet our current partying lifestyles can only change constructively if we can unite around a common cause, if we can find something to live for.

So where can we find the dream that addresses this crying need to talk the language of sustainability, that can feel fresh, and give hope? I am convinced that there is a dream within the scriptures that lies at the very heart of faith and is truly inspired by God. To introduce that I want to try to put what I have said so far into a biblical context.

## A biblical perspective on our current situation

I believe we are living in a prophetic age. Prophetic ages are marked by certain common themes. They are times of massive crisis in a society leading to radical change. They are marked by a sense that the old stories that have upheld the existing

........................................

3        Preface by Jonathan Porritt to *Permaculture in a Nutshell* by Patrick Whitefield 4th Edition Permanent Publications

culture no longer quite work, where prominent people seek to deny the crisis, and where the voice of truth comes from the margins.

There are two obvious examples of prophetic ages in the Bible. One is the time of the exile when the community of faith were carried away into a foreign land. The other is the time of Jesus when the people were under Roman Occupation. Both of these have interesting lessons for us as we enter our own prophetic age.

You may know something about the period of the exile in the Bible. It began with prophets like Jeremiah and first Isaiah warning people that the land would be overrun and the people taken away to a foreign land. Many did not want to hear their message. Jeremiah cried out to people that, if only they would change their ways, God would let them remain in the land. His life was threatened. His scrolls burnt. The people hardened their hearts and eventually they were, just as he had predicted, overrun by a foreign power. There were terrible scenes as the people were carried away. There were terrible agonies of faith later on as the people wondered what had become of God and God's promises to them as a people. Such is a prophetic age.

Likewise, in the New Testament, an immense crisis loomed. The people were suffering under Roman Occupation and there was a real threat of a Jewish uprising followed by a terrible Roman crackdown. There were also signs of the old stories no longer working. The Jewish people felt terribly compromised by the occupation. The Jewish law had become complex and had sometimes lost touch with its original purpose. The people were taxed into terrible poverty. Jesus saw the potential disaster as the swords were forged in Galilee to prepare for the uprising and called people to follow him on a different path. As he entered Jerusalem for the last time he cried out 'Would that even today you knew the things that make for peace'. But they would not hear. In AD69 the threatened Jewish revolt occurred, only to be savagely put down by Titus, together with the sacking of Jerusalem and the destruction of the Temple.

So what of today? Is this a similar prophetic age? I believe so. The environmental challenges that we are facing add up to a potential crisis greater than anything that has happened before on earth, eclipsing in impact the two biblical parallels above. It is a crisis that will be global in extent, affecting nations and people right across the earth, especially the world's poorest peoples. There may be social unrest on a scale never seen before, wars over resources, the extinction of creatures and changes in the earth's biosystems that last for centuries. And who are the prophets of this impending disaster? This time the warning is not the preserve of the religious, but is led by scientists, the UN's own Intergovernmental Panel on Climate Change. Yet, just like in other such ages, there are those who deny the crisis. There are oil companies who finance dissent. There are politicians who cannot bear the truth. And there are ordinary folk who simply find it all overwhelming.

So what will happen in our prophetic age? Who knows? But some things are clear. Jeremiah called the society of his day to 'amend your ways and your actions', saying that only then would God let them live in that land. [4] This was the heart of his message and it may be the heart of God's message today. There really is no alternative but to shift toward a life more in tune with the earth. Likewise, Jesus longed that people should learn 'the things that make for peace'. He lived with the prospect of serious social unrest. So do we. The changes

....................................................

4      Jeremiah 7 v 5-7

that are coming upon us will pit many against each other. Can we, even now, learn better ways to live?

We also desperately need to find a story to live by. It is clear that our philosophers, politicians and business people have all lost the plot. Unfortunately, the stories of the church are not working either. It is an uncomfortable truth that our churches, at least in the UK, are in crisis. The old stories no longer seem to have any traction. The traditions and ways of thinking that we have inherited no longer address the age in which we live. Instead many churches are turning in on themselves, more and more worried about building their own organisations and less and less concerned about any sense of purpose that serves the wider society. The 'environment' is perceived by many in this context as another burden, that needs to be quietly shoved aside, for the sake of a 'gospel' that is defined in other worldly terms[5].

There was a moment when Jeremiah felt called to go down to the house of a potter[6]. There he watched a man work the clay. He saw how sometimes the pot was spoiled in the potter's hands and he knocked the clay back and began again. And as he watched, the clay became a picture of the whole society being formed by God. 'Can I not do the same with you,' said God, as the pot was spoilt and the potter began again. Is that what God is going to have to do with this society in which we are living? Will God let it go and begin again? That must be a real possibility at this point. Or will we respond to the challenge before us, change our ways and begin to live radically different lives?

I sense society needs something that the Christian church could provide, but in order to do that we need to refresh

5       See Chapter 7 for further explanation of this
6       Jeremiah 18 v1 ff

our own story. There is something very tired about the way that Christians are talking about their faith and the Bible. Anachronistic concepts like 'stewardship' are not only from a different age, but they are scarcely present within the Bible itself, at least in the sense of stewardship of the earth. We need a fresh reading of the scriptures that conveys the authentic faith, but without the baggage that we have inherited. This book is an attempt to present an alternative, creation-centred, thematic approach to the whole of scripture.

This book is also part of a wider enterprise, which is to refresh the practice of Christian community and begin to live the dream. The movement is to be known as EarthAbbey.

Al Gore recently made a short film which ends with a new call. He said in effect, "I want you to see your life at this moment of earth history, not as a terrible burden, but as an enormous privilege. This may be one of the most important moments in human history. In hundreds of years' time the poets will speak of these days and the historians will write of them."

I think that is a great way of thinking, but what will they say of this generation? Did we respond? And what will they say of the church? Did it rise to the challenge? It is an awesome responsibility to be a shaper of earth's history.

## Chapter Two
# A Dream Arises

The old man Abraham stepped out from his tent in the evening of the day. All around him was evidence of God's blessing on his life. From the tents came the sound of laughter and music as the herdsman whiled away their evening. The dark shadows of his cattle stood in a quietness interrupted only by the occasional sound of a calf seeking refuge in its mother.

At times like this Abraham loved his life, moving as they did from one part of the country to another, always exploring, using all their knowledge and wisdom to discern where would be the best pasture, where would be the next water. A great tribe now depended on his decisions and he was grateful for the sense of God's hand on their lives. Only one thing nagged in his heart. The need for an heir. It had been many years now and how they had longed for a child. He looked up to the stars. It seemed as if there were more and more at each moment of his looking. It was then he felt the reassurance. 'Your descendants shall be as many as the stars in the sky.'

It is a beautiful tale from the very origins of biblical faith, from the days of the pastoralists who wandered the lands of Canaan. We have their names, Abraham, Isaac, Jacob. We read their stories of meetings with kings, relationships with kin, and worries over inheritance. Such people measured wealth in terms of increase in their cattle, their gold, and their offspring, and they were acutely aware of their dependence on the earth and its creatures. For them, faith was wrapped up in creation. The increase of their herds was the blessing of God and their skill in husbandry was the wisdom of God.

The Judaeo-Christian faith grew in such a context. These were people in touch with themselves, their ancestors, with the realities of life and with a deep sense of God. It seems that the natural world speaks of God. It may even be a primary source of faith.

As I conduct discussions around the country on creation, I often ask people to speak of a memorable time when they felt particularly in touch with nature. These groups have all sorts of people in them, but I am always astonished how these conversations immediately take on a spiritual tone. Eyes light up and you get a sense that people are speaking about something truly precious as they tell about the sunset on the shore or the wild patch of land they grew up with. This, I believe, was also the experience of the people of the scriptures. It is deep in us, part of our makeup. You could say it is part of the gift of God that we know God through nature.

In that sense it is hardly surprising that the most popular words of the Bible today are these:

*The Lord is my shepherd*
*I shall not want*
*He makes me lie down in green pastures*

*He leads me beside still waters*
*He restores my soul*

Psalm 23 speaks of nature as God's chosen means of healing for the human soul. Many people know that reality.

It is unfortunate that so many of us now live in cities. The process of urbanisation has advanced massively since the Industrial Revolution. In the UK something like 90% of people now live in towns and cities. Globally the figure is about 50% and rising. At one level we may enjoy our fast, choice-filled and glitzy city lifestyles, but at another we may long for something we are missing. That something is nature and the sense of God through nature. City living cuts us off from the realities of life. Few of us grow our own food anymore. It comes in plastic bags, ready washed. Few of us feel the cold anymore. We all have central heating. Light and dark are dealt with by electric lights. The refuse people take away our rubbish. And we are left out of touch with the earth.

In America they have a long established tradition of wilderness wandering. People go away as a group for weeks out into the wild. Some people have researched what happens when people go through this experience and they find that people not only enjoy themselves at a deep level, but that they often make major life strategy decisions while they are there. One study of 2000 wilderness wanderers found that 38% of these people made key life decisions during their trip, which were still in action five years later.[7] So it seems that the wilderness not only puts us in touch with God, but it can also change lives.

.................................................

7        Robert Greenway 'The Wilderness effect and ecopsychology'- chapter in *Ecopsychology* edited by Theodore Roszak, Mary Gomes and Allan Kamer 1995

That should not come as a surprise to readers of the Bible, of course, because many of the key people in the Bible, when faced with an important decision, went to the wild place. Think of Moses. After a royal upbringing, his heart was uneasy for his people. A moment's rage when a soldier was beating a Hebrew led to an exile in the wilderness. His life out in the hills and the desert brought him back in touch with himself and with God. The day came when he saw a bush that burned and heard a voice...and, as we say, the rest is history.

Or we might consider Elijah, the religious zealot, who had contended against Ahab and Jezebel and their godless ways for so long, who had confronted the prophets of Baal, whose life was at risk every day. When he was burnt out and demoralised, where did he go? To the wild place. To a brook with the ravens and then to the mountain where he heard the still small voice.

Then there was John the Baptist, a man with a reforming zeal, who sensed the need to see the world differently. He too went to the desert and submitted to its life, complete with a coat of camel hair and food of locusts and wild honey. There he met God and found the passion that would dare to cry out to the religious people of his day 'You brood of vipers, who warned you to flee from the wrath to come.'

In a different style, there was Jesus of Nazareth, who was to prepare himself for his years of ministry. He needed to face down his inner struggles and temptations and find the purity with which he could be true to his calling. And where did he go? To the wilderness.

So it was, that time after time the natural world was the source of healing, encounter with God and equipment for life for those who shaped the biblical story.

Yet this was not all. As people pondered creation and thought of God, a vision of the world-as-it should-be arose. This was a great God-given dream, not just of human beings living well, but of the whole creation at peace. This dream is found in snatches right through the biblical texts and I will introduce it to you in six themes.

## Rest

Rest is good, especially when you have completed a task. Sit down, feet up, satisfied. You know the feeling. Even after a great task, like creating the earth, rest is good. So the writer of the first chapter of Genesis gives us an account of creation that is actually structured around rest. We read that God rested on the seventh day and so blessed it. This story of creation became the primary reason given for a day of rest in biblical society. The intent was to give a space for reflection on life, a space to be with people and a space to restore the soul. The Sabbath was given as a gift to bless us and allow us to lift our eyes from the pressures of daily life to imagine the world as God would have it to be. We are fools to have been distracted into thinking about Sabbath as a set of rules for things you can't do. Each week the Sabbath would be like a celebration of the completion of creation. It may be that the primary task of any religion is to give its people space to imagine a better world. Such reflective space is certainly in short supply today as we work ever harder in our relentless pursuit of a wealth that is destroying the earth and our own souls. It's as if we have forgotten how to rest in a restorative way. We can pursue our interests, drive our cars to shopping malls, or zone out in front of the TV, but are we actually finding the healing and hope we crave? Biblical faith encouraged people to rest and so made space for dreaming. And a dream arose.

## Harmony

It is difficult to overemphasise how important the presence of nature was to the development of faith in the scriptures. Nature sank into their bones. It is still a commonplace among rural peoples around the world, that they watch the seasons, the rain, the flowers and the birds and they look for signs, knowing that the whole of life is one great network of inter-dependence, that strange things may spell danger and that some form of harmony is essential. Such a watching of the earth is clearly present in biblical minds. The writer of Psalm 104, for example, celebrates the creation, the springs that gush forth in the valleys, the grass growing for the cattle, the trees, the rain, the birds' nests, the mountains for the goats, the moon and the seasons, the lions and even humans get a mention(!) as they 'go forth to their work and their labour until the evening.' And for the psalmist it is God who makes all this happen, giving each plant and creature its place in the whole. All life was interconnected, and the greatest thing that one could ever hope for was to live in harmony with the rest of life on the planet.

Another psalm, Psalm 19, takes us on a whole step further. It is clearly the result of meditation (v 14) and begins by exalting God as proclaimed by nature.

*The heavens are telling the glory of God and the firmament proclaims his handiwork. Day to day pours forth speech, and night to night declares knowledge. There is no speech, nor are there words; yet their voice goes out through all the earth and their words to the end of the world.*

It likens the path of the sun to a bridegroom leaving his bed filled with the joys of his wedding night. Then it suddenly moves into what seems like new territory.

*The law of the Lord is perfect reviving the soul, the testimony of the Lord is sure making wise the simple...*

To us, this shift from the glories of the heavens to the law that ordered their society makes no sense, but to them it was obvious. The law of their society was built to reflect and be in harmony with the ordering of the natural world. They dreamt of living in harmony with God and that meant living in harmony with what God had created in nature. These two ideas were inseparably connected. How far we have strayed from this in our thinking today as we rape the earth, destroying its great forests, plundering its resources and polluting the skies. Colin Tudge is an agriculturalist, who has studied the way that modern farming has developed. He concludes that science is now used, not to work with nature, but to override it in the interests of profit[8]. This is an idea to which we shall return, but for now we simply notice that for the people of the Bible their dream was to live in harmony with God and creation.

### Fruitfulness

The people of the Bible, as you would expect of religious people, sensed the importance of doing what God required of them. But what was so interesting about their particular conception of this was the idea that they would know whether they were doing right by the very fruitfulness of the land. In the book of Deuteronomy, for example, we read

*And if you obey the Lord your God, being careful to do all his commandments that I command you this day....Blessed shall you be in the city, and blessed shall you be in the field. Blessed shall be the fruit of your body, and the fruit of your ground, and the fruit of your beasts, the increase of your*

..............................................

8        Colin Tudge *So shall we reap* Penguin 2004 p 175

*cattle and the young of your flock. Blessed shall be your basket and your kneading trough...*[9]

The link with the natural world is clear. Biblical spirituality was based on the premise that the primary sign of living well by God would be that their fields and their flocks would be fruitful. And the reverse was also true, namely 'If you will not obey the Lord your God...' there follows a list of warnings about consequences that includes the precise reverse of the blessings and throws in drought and disease for good measure[10]. Similar thought patterns can be found in Amos as he conceives the restoration of the society and God's favour in terms of the fruitfulness of the land[11].

Some might see the origin of this type of thinking in the basic intuition of the farmer who thanks God for a good harvest and worries about having offended God when times are hard. Some might say this way of thinking is primitive and pre-scientific and might respond with 'All we need is fertiliser, tractors, artificial insemination, antibiotics etc.' Such attitudes are about to appear for what they are, arrogance. As we have impoverished soils across the earth with our modern methods and polluted the air such that the very climate is changing, it is time to think again and recognise that there was something precious in such 'primitive' attitudes. The belief in a Creator is part of a great vision about the interdependence of all things. We mess with creation at our peril. And climate change should impress that upon us scientifically as well as theologically.

...............................................

9       Deuteronomy 28 v 1-5

10      Deuteronomy 28 v 15ff

11      Amos 3 v 18-19

## Trust

How should we relate to one another and to God? What is the best way to think of human society and human cooperation? The communities of the Bible saw life and their interrelationships as a trust. The big meaning of the first five books of the Bible is to lay out the 'trust' or the covenant between the people and God. It was real and practical but it was also intimate. People dreamt of a beautiful harmony between people and of a social situation where God would actually live among them. In Leviticus, for example, we read

*And I will make my home among you and my soul shall not abhor you. And I will walk among you and will be your God and you shall be my people[12].*

This was part of a vision for a just society, where at every level of life there were people who would care for those who fell on hard times. Among the poorest there was Ruth, the Moabitess, who left her own people and country to care for Naomi. Among the most privileged there was the King of Psalm 72 who had a duty to help the poor and deliver the needy person from the oppressor. And there was the truly compassionate judge conceived in Job, who says

*I was eyes to the blind, feet to the lame, a father to the poor and I searched out the cause of him I did not know. I broke the fangs of the unrighteous and made him drop his prey from his teeth...[13]*

All these tell of a society that dreamt of human flourishing and of a richness and justice in human relationships. This too was part of the dream.

..............................................

12      Leviticus 26 v 11-12

13      Job 29 v 15-17

## Celebration

People need to celebrate. Celebrations draw people together and help us stick together. They also provide a focus for the telling of stories and recognising what is important about life. It is no coincidence that many of the biblical celebrations focussed on the fruitfulness of the land. Here the people tasted the goodness of God, expressed their thanks to one another for joining together in the harvest and simply enjoyed being alive. There was the Feast of Weeks, celebrating the barley and wheat harvest, the Feast of Booths, which followed the harvesting of summer fruit like dates, figs and pomegranates, and the feast of Passover which celebrated their deliverance from Egypt and God's provision for them in the wilderness. These three great pilgrim festivals involved a journey to Jerusalem and were the occasion of celebration and singing. A whole set of psalms known as the songs of 'ascent' were sung at the time of 'going up' to Jerusalem. Moments of celebration are also moments of reflection, of giving thanks for the past and dreaming of the future. Celebration was part of the dreaming.

## Peace

There was a need for peace, but the people dreamt of more than simply the absence of violence between humans. Isaiah offered them hope in these terms[14]

*A shoot shall come forth from the stump of Jesse,*
*And a branch shall grow out of his roots*
*And the spirit of the Lord shall rest upon him,*
*The spirit of wisdom and understanding...*
*...he shall not judge by what his eyes see*
*Or decide by what his ears hear;*

......................................................

14     Isaiah 11 v 1-9

*But with righteousness he shall judge the poor*
*And decide with equity with the meek of the earth...*

And this message of the coming peace extended even to the creatures. He goes on in some of the most beautiful words in all scripture

*The wolf shall dwell with the lamb*
*And the leopard shall lie down with the kid*
*And the calf and the lion and the fatling together*
*And a little child shall lead them.*
*The cow and the bear shall feed*
*And their young shall lie down together*
*And the lion shall eat straw like an ox.*
*The suckling child shall play over the hole of the snake*
*And the weaned child shall put his hand in the adder's den.*

Realists among us might scoff at lion eating straw like an ox and shrink away from these strange pictures of our creatures, but what Isaiah was trying to express was the dream for a radical new type of peace, necessitating even a new type of creation. The passage is summed up by a great hope for non-violence in all life.

*They shall not hurt or destroy in all my holy mountain;*
*For the earth shall be full of the knowledge of the Lord as the*
*waters cover the sea.*

Such are the themes – rest, harmony, fruitfulness, trust, celebration and peace and a few of the passages that illustrate them. But we should not view these themes as separate. They belong together. They are actually about the one dream and sometimes they are found like that. As in Micah

*It shall come to pass in the latter days*
*That the mountain of the house of the Lord*
*shall be raised up*

*And all the peoples shall flow to it...*
*They shall beat their swords into ploughshares*
*And their spears into pruning hooks*
*Nation shall not lift up sword against nation*
*Neither shall they learn war any more*
*But they shall sit everyone under their vine*
*and under their fig tree*
*and none shall make them afraid.*

Here we see the themes of rest, celebration, trust, peace, fruitfulness and harmony all intermingling in a dream of the future. For those people this was the dream they would call 'Shalom' and which would express that greater peace and harmony of all life that they longed for.[15] It was a complete realisation of God's purposes for human beings, as people fulfilling their potential, both individually and as members of their communities, living in a just and harmonious order, without fear or threat.

........................................

15        Some readers may be concerned about the favouring of Israel over against other nations implied by this passage. This is considered in Chapter 4.

## Chapter Three

# Recognising ourselves

One of the great challenges of today is to describe in ordinary language what people are in relation to God, each other and the rest of creation. Such big picture ideas form the way that we see the world. They form a bed of largely unconscious assumptions about the way that we live. Part of what we mean by our environmental problems being a spiritual disease is that we need to rethink the big ideas.

People have been wondering about what we really *are* for a long time, right back into biblical times. It was a continual source of meditation for them as it is for us today. And I think there may have been something of a common thread in their reflections. For the biblical communities that wrote about this, human nature can be summed up in two words.

The first word is extraordinary. Right down through the ages human beings have looked at what they have achieved, perhaps in a great building, or bridge, or piece of agriculture and they have sensed that they are special. The writer of Psalm 8 wonders about these human beings who seem 'little less than God', are crowned with 'glory and honour' and seemed to have such power over the rest of creation.

At the same time the world stubbornly refuses to revolve around human beings and, when the people of faith thought they understood God and expected God to micromanage the world according to their ideas of justice, they had a terrible lesson to learn. The book of Job ends with this sort of hard lesson for Job and his advisors (Chapter 38ff). They thought they understood how to avoid suffering and poverty, instead, the sheer wildness of creation was to teach them humility before the God of all the earth.[16]

So being 'extraordinary' does not free us from all constraints. This brings us to the second word that describes human nature in the Bible. And that is frustration.

Let me show you how these go together in two seminal biblical passages. The first is the story of the building of the tower of Babel in Genesis 11. The people decide to build an extraordinary city and a tower with its 'top reaching to the heavens' in order to 'make a name for themselves'. God sees this and fears that soon 'nothing will be impossible for them.' And we read of the giving of many languages as a deliberate strategy to 'frustrate' the development of human beings, confusing their speech and scattering them across the earth. I hope you will agree that this is obviously a story with a meaning, rather than anything historical. But we can imagine it arising from this ancient civilisation, which was indeed building great cities, encountering other nations with different languages and experiencing the frustrations and misunderstandings that go with that. Yet it is also a deeper reflection on human nature. We do reach for the sky. We do have a tendency to imagine that we can do anything. We are an extraordinary

........................................................

16      More on this in Chapter 9

people. And yet we need to be humbled also. Extraordinary frustration combine together to make a phrase that I suspect we all recognise.

## Revisiting the garden

'Extraordinary frustration' is also the key to understanding, what I think may be the most misunderstood story of all time. And that is the story of the Garden of Eden in Genesis chapter 2 and 3. I believe this story to be similar in type to that of the tower of Babel. It is a reflection on the human condition, on the fact that we find ourselves in a situation of extraordinary power and yet are frustrated at every turn in our attempts to put our dreams into practice. And it may be very unhelpful to cast this story as 'The Fall'. Let me explain.

I think this story is a story of origins like the tower of Babel. It also carries a deep meaning for us, and revolves around the two abiding facets of human experience, 'extraordinary' and 'frustration'. It is important to recognise that this story is thought to originate independently of Genesis 1 so when we read it we should read it as an account of our origins that stands on its own. It does not 'know' the stuff about being created in God's image, for example, from Genesis 1. The writer is trying to explain the human condition as from nothing. Hence it begins in Genesis 2 v 4b with an earth that is bare, without plants or animals. A mist (or flood) comes up from the earth and God forms the human out of dust from the ground and breathes the breath of life into those first nostrils. It is an evocative picture which is then filled in with the formation of the beautiful garden, with the great rivers flowing from it and connecting with the minerals and other treasures of the earth. And the human is told to till and keep the garden, but not to touch two of the trees or eat their fruit.

So far it is a simple tale with a mystical twist. The two special trees are presented as potential sources of something both great and terrible. They are sources of the 'extraordinary'. They are, in the writers view, a picture of how humans *became* extraordinary.

Then we have the delightful making and naming of the creatures and the differentiation of man and woman and their coming together. Followed by the crunch, as the apple is eaten, the deed is discovered and the curse is given. I believe that in the eating of the apple from the tree of the knowledge of good and evil, we have two things. And it is vital to recognise them both. Firstly we have human beings becoming extraordinary. As it says, 'when you eat of it, your eyes will be opened, and you will be like God, knowing good and evil'. Such 'knowing' is usually understood to imply our capacity to do things, so that human beings become able to do all sorts of things like develop agriculture, gunpowder, or nuclear energy and that these capacities can be used either for good or for evil. This was the story of us attaining to the extraordinary capacities that we know so well today.

And its giving was coupled to frustration. The cursings, that follow from the crunch of the apple, span, in metaphorical terms, the great frustrations of the human condition. We may dream of harmony with the creatures of the earth (2 v 19) but in practice we find enmity and struggle between us – as figured in the woman and the snake (3 v 15). We may dream of a simple fruitfulness like that of the trees (2 v 9), but in practice our own reproduction is painful (3 v 16) and working the land is tough (3 v 17-19). We may dream of easy relationships, but these are so often confounded by our deep desires (3 v 16) and by abusive power relations (3 v 16). We may dream of living for ever (3 v 22) but our mortality is all too evident (3 v 19). We might expect an easy and evident knowledge of God

(3 v 8) but somehow the way seems barred and we know but glimpses (3 v 24)

So this story gives us a way to reflect on the two basic facets of human nature and depicts their origin through this dramatic tale. I am proposing that the narrative elements of this tale are essentially dramatic devices that serve the big project of this story which is to explain what we are. The story begins with the human being in the harmonious garden tending the soil, but this is not humanity as we know it now. They were neither *extraordinary nor frustrated*.

Most stories, and indeed most biblical stories, can be read in several ways. Different ways of reading them draw out different meanings and these can complement one another rather than exclude each other. This story has traditionally been described as 'The Fall' and is usually set as an integral part of the great drama of salvation that begins creation, fall, redemption etc. There is no doubt that it is used in this way by Paul in the New Testament and it has probably become as important as it has simply because it is used as the backdrop to the redemptive work of Christ.

What I am suggesting here is that this description may be valid at one level, but that the words 'The Fall' cause us to focus on certain elements of the story like the temptation, disobedience and casting out from the garden and shut out alternative ways of reading that may have been much nearer the original intent and meaning of the first author. I think that in the mind of the person who wrote it this story was not primarily a moral tale, nor was it about temptation. It was about transition. It was the story of human beings going from an imagined, naive, relatively impotent, but harmonious state, to the state they find themselves in today with all their potential and all their frustrations.

The garden, of course, is a picture of the great peace, that harmony that people of every age have dreamt of, with the natural fruitfulness of the earth, a harmony of relations with animals, peace with one another and with God. The only difference is that the human beings in this story did not yet have the same capacities that we have, nor indeed the frustrations. Adam and Eve were not 'extraordinary'nor filled with 'frustration' in the way that we have described it.

Thinking about who and what we are also has to consider Genesis 1. This opening chapter of the Bible is fascinating because its hymn of creation is wholly positive about human beings. Beginning from an earth 'without form and void' we are drawn with great beauty through the formation of the earth. We notice that this creation was to a large extent an ongoing process, even at this stage. One thing was made out of another. The waters were to 'bring forth' the living creatures of the sea'. The earth was to 'bring forth' the animal life. And on the sixth day we read something special happened in that God said 'Let us make human beings in our image'. And we are told that this means 'after our likeness' and that these creatures will somehow attain power over all the rest. This story is, in the terms that we have been using, another account of human beings becoming 'extraordinary'.

So what are we to make of all this? I want to notice first that all this stuff is incredibly accurate. Human beings are special. Some of us wince today at the words about having dominion over the other creatures, particularly since Christians have been accused of using this to justify the abuse of the earth and its creatures. In fact, our problems with climate change and the environment may have much more to do with the absence of proper faith-inspired reflection on life during the last two hundred years. Over this period we have seen religion deliberately pushed out of the public square in favour of the ideology of the free market and apparent 'rationalism'. These things are probably the true cause of our earth destructive mindset today. The biblical words about human dominion over the creatures of the earth should probably be seen more as a statement of fact. They are a recognition of the actual state of things, a call to recognise our responsibility and accept our power.[17]

## Thinking of ourselves as creative creatures

Let me try to sum the argument up so far in a description of who and what we are as human beings. I propose that we consider ourselves to be creative creatures.

If we consider each of these words in turn, the word creative is my choice description of that aspect of our nature that I have called so far 'extraordinary'. There are many different ways that one can think of the special nature of human beings. We could cite our abilities with language, our imagination, our ability to reason, or even our capacity for faith. We could think of how these work out into our ability to tell stories or explore science, to dream of better worlds or to search after God. But I think it is interesting to think of ourselves as specially 'creative'. By creative I don't mean the 'good-with-fuzzy-felt' sort of creative, but rather something much deeper and more profound.

Terence Fretheim[18] has pointed out that creation in the bible is seen in at least three ways, an originating creation, an ongoing creation and an ultimate creation. He proposes that the idea

...............................................

17      The attitude that I am referring to is obvious in Psalm 8, which offers very similar words about dominion, but the tone is most obviously one of humility

18      Terence Fretheim, *God and the world in the Old Testament – a relational theology of Creation*. Abingdon Press 2005

of God continuing creation in an ongoing sense is much more important than we have realised. We should think not only of the physical attributes of the earth as being formed by God, but also that human beings have acted as co-creators in the world on their own account and that our politics, our social systems and relationships are all indeed part of creation. In fact this is the essence of what we call theism. God continues to act in the world and one of the most important ways that God acts is through human beings as co-creators. Once you see this it shouts at you from the scriptures. In Isaiah 43, for example, the prophet speaks of the great creator 'sending to Babylon' and 'breaking down the bars' to release the people[19]. In other places Isaiah speaks of God 'stirring up one from the East'[20] to deliver the people. Likewise God is said to be 'grasping the right hand of Cyrus'[21] through whom these people are to be delivered. When Isaiah says of God in Chapter 43 'Behold I do a new thing, now it springs forth...'[22]he is speaking of the social and historical change to do with the return of the people to their land, yet the words in their original language are those applied to an act of creation. All these phrases point to the biblical idea that God is working with human beings to make new things happen in the world and, in that sense, creation is continuing.

This leads to the idea that human beings are 'creative' in the sense that they make history. They co-create with God. That is part of what makes us special. Once we recognise this we need to also recognise that we are meaning here not just human history, which is tragically how we currently think,

.................................................

19      Isaiah 43 v 14

20      Isaiah 41 v 2

21      Isaiah 45 v 1

22      Isaiah 43 v 19

but rather that we have the capacity to shape *earth* history. It is the whole creation that is in view.

If this is the case, then the task of the religious person in this, as in every age, is to search to understand how God is working and then do God's work. That is what Isaiah and all the prophets of the scriptures were trying to discern. They were not always sure. Their differing accounts enrich our understanding of God's will even as the story of Christ brought their ideas to a glorious fulfilment. Yet they were about the same business that we must be about. We must try to discern God's hand in the earth today. I shall argue later in the book why I believe God to be at work in the environmental movement, but, as a taste, I invite you to consider the extraordinary growth in public awareness about the environment that we have experienced in the last five years. Where has it come from? Is this the Spirit of God? If so, this must be a challenge to the disciples of Christ. Surely we must try to be people who do the work of God, shaping earth's history for God today? And I believe that means we must seek a new peace with the earth, a new harmony with the natural world in accordance with the great dream of the Bible. This brings us to the second category of our description for we are surely also 'creatures'.

The aspect of human nature that we have called 'frustration' can now largely be traced to our inheritance as creatures. We are laden with the deep level emotions and desires of creatures. We work with, and suffer from, power structures like other animal hierarchies. We long for sex and are consumed with jealousy. We suffer from pain, and sickness and death. We love our families and our local groups and fear the stranger. All these things are actually the common property of what we call higher creatures. Their presence in our minds can be traced to evolutionary pressures. And they are part of both the richness of human existence and its frustration.

It is also true that much human activity can be understood as the behaviour of a creature which seeks to establish its niche on the earth. Every creature seeks to command a habitat. Every creature works and works hard for their basic livelihood. Are humans any different in this respect? As we spend our energies on our homes with our visits to the DIY warehouse and the choosing of carpets and curtains, are we doing anything substantially different from the bird who builds its nest? As we rear our children and defend them at all costs, are we doing anything substantially different from any other creature with deep motivations to reproduce? The difference is that we have become so successful in reproduction and controlling our habitat that we have spread throughout the world, commanding its resources and potentially bringing about a crisis in the earth itself. Of course, lots of animals overbreed in their own small corners and then suffer crises where huge numbers die, but humans are now everywhere and their impact so great that their crisis will threaten most other life on the planet. By polluting the atmosphere, destroying the rainforests and melting the icecaps, we are like Samson pulling down the great building upon ourselves as we die. That would be a sad end, and perhaps it does not have to be like that. Maybe the first step on our journey of change will be to embrace our creatureliness.

When Darwin first announced his theory of evolution the real scandal was not the theory itself but the terrible insinuation that we came from apes. This was too much for Bishop Wilberforce. Human beings in Wilberforce's age had learnt to think of themselves as a cut above the other creatures, so different as to live their lives in a completely separate sphere. Yet the truth is now clear. We are creatures and we need to relearn our creatureliness. We are dependent on the earth and its creatures as they are dependent on us. Joanna Macy says that what we need is a 'great turning' and this will involve both a new sense of interconnectedness between humans and the rest of life on the earth and a new sense of compassion for the earth and its creatures. There are some signs that this is happening. For example there is currently an upsurge in interest in wildlife. *Springwatch* and such shows have mass audiences. Likewise, David Attenborough has become one of the most trusted voices of our generation and an icon of education about the natural world. One of the most encouraging features of Christian influence in environmentalism has been the celebration of the creatures of the earth and active management of ecosystems for our mutual good. The long standing work of A Rocha is a prime example.

So what are we? I contend that we are creative creatures and that this should lead us to an enormous empathy and sense of connection with the earth and all life, but also impress upon us a powerful weight of responsibility as a result of our ability to shape earth history.

To conclude this chapter, I ask that we revisit the garden one last time, this time to consider the other tree, known as the tree of life. In Christian understanding this tree of life has come to be seen as symbolic of Christ, but I suggest that the original author may have made another connection that is also worthy of attention. In Genesis, God expels Adam and Eve from the garden out of an apparent fear that they might eat of the tree of life and live forever. (Gen 3 v 22) The original source of this idea might actually be traced to Proverbs where we read

*Happy is the one who finds wisdom...*
*She is more precious than jewels...*
*Long life is in her right hand...*

*She is a tree of life to those who lay hold of her;* [23]

To live well as a creative creature is a formidable task and the space between the dreams of our extraordinary minds and the frustrations of our creaturehood needs to be filled with the search for wisdom. How can we order our lives so as to work well for the great dream of peace? How can we overcome our simple rapacious behaviour upon the earth? The challenge is to find wisdom, the tree of life.

.................................................

23      Prov 3 v 18

# Chapter Four
# The dream goes global

Our world may be warming up to serious conflict. The Cold War may be over, but a new one is about to begin. This time it will be about energy security. It is clear already that some countries will refuse to adapt to life without cheap oil. Instead they will fight to preserve their 'freedom' to live as they choose. This will put them on a collision course with other powerful nations who will be doing the same. Many people have discerned something of the need to protect oil supplies in the decision to invade Iraq, the sabre rattling towards Iran or the stand off over Georgia. This sort of strategic thinking runs deep in our history. Today it is particularly being expressed in terms of rights to drill under the emerging seas of the Arctic ice cap. There are international laws about land under the sea with complex proofs about whether or not it is an extension of your own continental shelf etc, but the reality on the ground is that there is most likely to be a power play for these and other similar resources. They are perceived as too important.

Human beings, of course, have always been involved in tribal disputes of one form or another. One of the more disturbing things about the dream of peace in the Bible is that it was originally cast in tribal, or more precisely, national terms. It was about Israel over against the rest of the world. For some people this casts a shadow over the reading of the scriptures, but there is another way of thinking about this. The uncomfortable truth is that all the terrible things that the Bible records about tribal mentalities are still happening in the world of today. We can either stand aloof from these stories and say how awful they are or we can seek to learn from them. In particular we can see how belief in God eventually transcended this way of thinking and offered a global vision for peace. Let me try to explain what I mean.

The piece in Micah and Isaiah about 'beating swords into ploughshares and spears into pruning hooks', which concluded Chapter Two, all looks very fine until one faces the fact that this was a picture of all the nations coming to God in Zion – which meant Israel. This was part and parcel of a worldview which expected God to favour Israel and thereby beat down their enemies when necessary. Israel's perspective on life at this time includes terrible visions of God trampling Israel's enemies 'in my wrath' with clothes stained with their 'lifeblood' in a 'great day of vengeance'.[24] Such attitudes sadly remain and religious expressions of it are still found in the Middle East. Yet there is another way of telling the biblical story. And that is as a story of the way this attitude was eventually displaced by a global vision.

## One God over all the earth

The seeds of this new vision were sown in the very conception of a God who was one God and therefore implicitly the God of all. This idea was subversive of all expressions of tribal mentality. Belief in the one God was surely part of what ini-

...................................................

24      Isaiah 63 v 1-4

tially drew the twelve tribes of Israel together, but it could not allow them to stop there. It was an idea that must eventually be offered to the world. The potential for Israel to claim special favours of God, for example, was always in an uneasy tension with their belief in a God who was necessarily the God of all. This came to a crisis during the age of the exile. Living in a foreign land meant having to face the reality of other cultures and people and caused them to ask all sorts of questions about their narrower view of the world. It was probably at this time that their prophets began to think explicitly in terms of the great Creator.

The author of the second section of Isaiah begins his writings with a majestic vision of God[25], and a salvation which would be revealed to 'all flesh'- meaning everything in all creation. We were all in the same boat. 'All flesh is grass', he said. We would all go the same way. The nations were as nothing before God. They are like 'a drop from a bucket and are accounted as dust in the scales'. The leaders of nations are nothing. 'Scarcely are they planted, scarcely sown, scarcely has their stem taken root in the earth, when God blows upon them and they wither...'. So the writer sets the scene for the great work of God, the salvation of the earth and the coming of the one who will 'feed his flock like a shepherd, will gather the lambs in his arms.. and gently lead those who are with young'. This is a massive global vision and a beautiful one at that. And we can see in it the threads of a faith that would eventually transcend tribal mentalities and look for a peace that would be established across the earth.

### Heaven

This hope was encouraged further by another development to do with heaven. The idea of heaven did not arise, as we

...............................................

25      Isaiah 40

might imagine today, from contemplation of life after death. It actually came from an inspiration and a frustration. Let me explain. The people of the biblical communities believed in a God who was active in the world. That was the heart of what we call theism. And one great problem with such a belief was to explain why God did not do more to change the world. They dreamt of a world made right, of this great 'Shalom', and of a God who wanted such a world, so why did God not intervene and make it so? As they pondered this, you can imagine their eyes would go to the heavens and they would envisage God enthroned, looking down on them. When they write of this, we should not judge their words against our modern scientific concepts, but accept it as the language of dreams and truth of a different kind. The heavens spoke to them of God and the home of God as in Psalm 19

*The heavens are telling the glory of God*

Or Psalm 103

*The Lord has established his throne in the heavens and his kingdom rules over all*

There are a huge number of examples of this type of thinking[26]. The heavens became a focus for imagination and dreaming of what the world could and should be like.

*Thy steadfast love is great above the heavens[27]*

Some would cry out with frustration that God did not intervene more obviously in the world.

--------------------------------------------------

26      For example Ps 57 v 4,11; Ps 108 v 5; Ezra 9 v 6, 73 v 9; Ps 108 v 4; Ps 155 v 3, v 16; Isaiah 40 v 22; Ezek 1 v 1; Matthew 3 v 16; Matt 5 v 34

27      Psalm 108 v 4

People longed for God to intervene on behalf of the poor[29] or to help them personally[30] or to give them justice over their enemies.[31] So it was that the natural vision of 'the heavens', which any of us can see on a clear night, became the focus of a dream of 'heaven', which now meant what the world might be like and all that people hoped for in God. It was the imagination of a situation where God was fully known and God's will was done. It was also about a hope that God would one day break into the world and establish the peace of all. And, of course, such an idea had to give rise to a faith that ultimately would be truly global in extent.

## Jesus grasps the vision

Now let me skip forward some hundreds of years and to a young man in Nazareth who grew up studying such scriptures. We are used to thinking about Jesus through the eyes of the church, or via our various traditions or the New Testament epistles. This means we have to peer through layers of creeds and formulations, church history and doctrines that may cloud our view. I am going to suggest that we take a look at Jesus from a different angle and ask the question 'What inspired Jesus?' This is to try, as far as we can[32], to enter the

..................................................

28      Isaiah 64 v 1

29      Psalm 113

30      Psalm 57 v 3

31      Isaiah 64 v 1

32      Some will argue that any attempt to discern the mind of Jesus is doomed from the start, because so much what we have in the gospels results from impenetrable layers of interpretation. Tom Wright clearly does not take this view. Whatever position you take on this, the text that follows clearly show that the gospels betray the influence of Shalom thinking on the earliest understandings of Jesus words and actions.

mindset of Jesus from within his world and from the scriptures that he would have had access to. My principal guide in this venture has been Tom Wright and his book *Jesus and the Victory of God*. Tom Wright maintains that Jesus understood himself as in the line of the Old Testament prophets. This is obvious from parables like the Tenants in the Vineyard[33] or in the heartfelt cry as he entered Jerusalem for the last time;

*O Jerusalem, Jerusalem, killing the prophets and stoning those who are sent to you! How often would I have gathered you children together as a hen gathers her brood under her wings and you would not![34]*

Tom Wright suggests that the defining theme for Jesus' own self-understanding was that he saw himself as fulfilling the great hopes of the prophets for all that would happen in the joyous return from exile.

We can be sure that Jesus deeply engaged with the writings of Isaiah, Jeremiah and others. For example, in the great despair surrounding the parable of the sower, we sense the frustrations of prophetic work and Jesus' own awareness of directly fulfilling Isaiah's words,

*You shall indeed hear but never understand, you shall indeed see but never perceive.[35]*

Likewise, there can be little doubt that Jesus took up the writings of the prophets and transformed them according to his vision of God and his calling. He took Isaiah's Song of the

---

33 Luke 20 v 9-16

34 Matthew 23 v 37 see also the preceding verses which explain the context

35 Matthew 13 v 14 and Isaiah 6 v 9

Vineyard[36] and turned it into his own story about the tenants in the vineyard[37] and his meditation on the vine[38]. Some also believe that the prodigal son story is a reworking of Isaac, Jacob and Esau[39]. But what of the dream for harmony with the earth and its creatures? What part did this play in this thinking?

I love to think of Jesus poring over Isaiah, coming across the words about the coming one as the Prince of Peace[40] who would bring in a whole new situation where 'of the increase of his government and of peace there would be no end.'[41] Or, I think of Jesus wondering about his own calling as he read;

*How beautiful on the mountains are the feet of him who
brings good tidings
Who publishes peace
Who brings good tidings of good
Who publishes salvation
Who says to Zion 'Your God reigns'*[42]

I can sense Jesus' heart beginning to bang as he read those words, the excitement rising up within him as he recognised that God was calling him to bring the good news, that it was about 'Your God reigns' or, as he would say, 'the kingdom of God' or 'the kingdom of heaven' and central to this good news was the publishing of 'peace', that glorious shalom vision of

..................................................

36      Isaiah 5 v 1-7

37      Matthew 21 v 33ff

38      John 15

39      The basis for this is the shared themes, an inheritance is taken, the inheritor goes away, eventually makes for home, is worried about the reception and eventually there is a joyful reunion.

40      Isaiah 9 v 6

41      Isaiah 9 v 7

42      Isaiah 52 v 7

the world made right, the fulfilment and healing of individuals and communities, where there would be a new wholeness of life and a well-being, that includes social justice and the harmony of creation.

So in this seminal passage from Isaiah we have a cluster of interconnected ideas that may well have shaped Jesus understanding of his role. Key words and phrases like 'Good News', 'Kingdom of God', 'Kingdom of Heaven' and 'Peace' that Jesus used throughout his ministry can be traced to this source. And the root of all of them is in the dream of the world made right, the breaking in of God into the world, establishing, as he would say, 'your will be done on earth as it is in heaven'.

## Jesus proclaims the dream

The way that people are written about varies from culture to culture and age to age. In Jesus' time the equivalent of our biography would be a record of someone in terms of words and deeds. They would record their teaching, but they would also record what they did. In this way the things they did in their life were expected to reflect who they were at a deep level. We may find some of the stories of what Jesus did difficult to deal with today with our scientifically trained minds. We may not know quite what to do with the exorcism of an epileptic, or the rubbing on of mud to cure blindness. But let me invite you as reader to engage in a thought experiment. Try for a moment to put aside your concerns and just look at the gospel stories as stories for a moment. Then ask, 'What was their central message?' Jesus was clearly proclaiming some good news through what he did. Let's think about what the gospels record in terms of Jesus' actions. For example:

- The stilling of the storm
- Water into wine
- Feeding the crowd

- Cleansing of lepers
- Casting out demons
- Raising the dead
- Healing the sick
- Death and resurrection

Do you notice how many of these miracles were associated with some sort of impact on the natural world? More than that, do you see what type of impact this was? We may be familiar with interpreting Jesus' words and actions in terms of the compassionate love of God, social inclusion, addressing injustice and shaking the political world. But have we missed this great message about the renewal or healing of nature? The human social dimension was clearly an important part of the good news, but the really big picture within which all this sits is the message of the transformation of creation and a peace which would embrace the whole natural order. Jesus was fulfilling the dream.

If this is true then it ought to be reflected in Jesus teaching as well as his actions. So let's examine Jesus' teaching in the light of the six themes identified in Chapter Two.

## Rest

There are clear signs that Jesus was concerned to help people rest and find space to reflect on life. One of the most famous of his sayings goes,

*Come to me all who labour and are heavy laden and I will give you rest. Take my yoke upon you and learn from me for my yoke is easy and my burden is light and you will find rest for your souls.*

They are beautiful words, but so out of kilter with most of our current lifestyles. What is this vision for 'an easy yoke' and a 'burden that is light'? These words are profoundly countercultural in our ever more anxious and hectic society. Jesus had a vision for rest and for contemplation that we need. It was part of the dream. The same theme arose in the conversation with his friends Mary and Martha in Bethany. These two sisters lived together. One was busy serving Jesus, while the other sat at his feet and listened. Jesus commended Mary for her quietness and attentiveness. Mary was said to have made the good choice. There was rest at the heart of Jesus vision.

The New Testament writers, who followed Jesus, were also keen to emphasise that we would not find peace with God through busyness. They told of the grace of God through Christ freely given and invited people to simply enter that rest[43].

### Harmony and fruitfulness

As he wandered the fields of Galilee, Jesus pointed to the nature all around them

*See the birds of the air, they neither sow nor reap, not gather into barns yet your heavenly Father feeds them. Are you not of more value than they?..*

*Consider the lilies of the field, how they grow, they neither toil nor spin, nor gather into barns yet I tell you even Solomon in all his glory was not clothed like one of these...[44]*

For Jesus this was all part of a lesson in dependence on God and against getting anxiously caught up in the pursuit of money, status and material goods. Jesus understood all the living systems of the earth as caught up in a vital dependence on one another and through which the graciousness of the loving heavenly Father was expressed. He wanted us to feel

.................................................

43      The writer of the letter to the Hebrews takes up this theme

44      Matthew 6 v 26 and 28

the reality of the prayer 'Give us this day our daily bread'. He appealed to people to enter into that care through faith. For Jesus the very life of the disciples was to be conceived as fruit bearing. He was the vine. They were the branches. They were to be pruned and renewed as they bore fruit[45]. As we shall see below, this was more than a metaphor for Jesus. It was how he conceived the world. Jesus was revealing his own vision for a harmonious and fruitful earth with which we are vitally interconnected.

## Trust

Jesus own community is to model a new way of being, which includes an intimate knowing of one another[46] and a radical dependence on God through both the natural world and the wider community[47]. They are to eschew status and privilege and deliberately include outsiders and outcast. As a lesson in leadership he reaches for a child and says

*Whoever humbles himself like this child is the greatest in the kingdom of heaven (Matthew 18 v 2).*

In these things he is proclaiming the dream. And the first disciples knew this, as they too experimented with new ways of living, sharing their possessions and giving generously to those in need[48].

......................................

45      John 15

46      John 15 v 12

47      This is the deep meaning of the command to take little with them on their travels (Luke 9v3). They are to be cast on the mercy of others and experience the graciousness of God through the fruitfulness of nature (Matthew 6 v 25ff).

48      Acts 4 v 32ff

## Celebration

Jesus caused something of a kerfuffle by his partying. He would party with anyone. He saw it as a great way of relating to people. He also clearly took the main celebration days of his people very seriously and his death was mystically associated with a retelling of the Passover. Gathering his disciples for his last supper with them, he used that moment to prepare them for his death and resurrection and to re-imagine the story so vividly and powerfully that it would become a source of celebration for thousands of years, encouraging later disciples to work together to bring about the dream.

## Peace

Peace was a word whose meaning embraced all these themes and, as we have seen, so many of Jesus miracles. Jesus went about making peace and the big theme that embraced these actions was the renewal of creation. For Jesus, peace was something that needed to be made. It was not going to just happen. He needed to *do* peace, to make it, even against opposition. This was the core element of his proclamation. After his death, his poignant words to the disciples were 'Peace be with you' as he breathed the Spirit of God upon them and empowered them to continue the work of living and proclaiming the dream[49].

So it was that Jesus expressed the dream that had arisen so many centuries before him. He dreamt of the world as it might be, of God being fully known and of people living in harmony with one another and with the rest of creation. And his life was spent working to make that dream a reality. We have seen how Jesus built his teaching from the great global visions of Isaiah and it is not surprising then that it was through Jesus that these ideas were to transcend their

..............................................

49      John 20 v 19ff

tribal and national origins and become a dream for the whole earth. Jesus was the prime mover in making this transition, but it was a process that would not be completed until after his death when people began to reflect on the meaning and significance of what he had achieved.

## Chapter Five

# The seed that fell into the earth

Jesus knew that he had a special role to play in making the dream real and those who wrote about him were to make this explicit. Jesus did not just teach *about* this peace which was to embrace the whole creation. He did not just *do* things that brought peace to people and creation. Jesus is portrayed in the gospels as the unique source of this *Shalom* that was breaking into the world. His more extravagant words and actions like commanding 'Peace' to the storm on the lake or in describing himself as the 'Bread of Life' to the hungry multitudes around Galilee, these proclaim Jesus as something extraordinary with regard to the coming of this Shalom. He was somehow making it real in his person. But how are we to understand this?

For several years now I have been seeking a new way of understanding what Christ achieved. I am deeply aware that Christian proclamation as it stands today is almost entirely human-centred. We are told that Christ came to offer us forgiveness, that he died in our place, that our calling is to join this human community and live a life of sharing the good news. This is all very well but I have come to see that it is very 'thin'. It is not so much wrong as inadequate, because it fails to make any significant connections with the creation or with what it means to live well outside of 'church'.

I want to try to put forward a constructive suggestion that might at least lie alongside the current understandings. It concerns 'the seed that fell into the earth'.

As we have already seen Isaiah chapter 40 is a key passage for setting the work of God in a global, creation-centred frame. Within it lie these phrases – which, as I shall show, became a rich source of meditation for the writers of the New Testament and even for Jesus himself.

*All flesh is grass*
*And all its beauty like the flower of the field.*
*The grass withers and the flower falls*
*When the breath of the Lord falls upon it.*
*Surely the people is grass.*
*The grass withers and the flower fades;*
*But the word of our God will stand for ever.*[50]

Here is a picture of the fragility of all life, or all 'flesh'. The natural cycle of birth, decay and death is figured in terms of the seed of a flower and it is contrasted with a mysterious 'word of God' that will stand for ever.

Jesus' stories were actually full of this word picture. Some have simply put this down to his contact with and love for the natural world, but I suggest it might be more than this. I suggest that the idea of 'the seed that fell into the earth' was a primary source of understanding of the work of Christ

.................................................
50      Isaiah 40 v 6-8

both by the person of Jesus himself and by those who tried to understand the meaning of his life later.

## The seed and the word in Jesus teaching

For example, consider the parable of the sower. This is not just a parable. It is the parable about parables and the story that summarised Jesus' life's work. And it was couched in terms of 'a sower who went out to sow' and one whose seeds were 'the word'. A more explicit link with Isaiah would be hard to imagine. Jesus' work was, like the prophets before him, a deliberate sowing of seed. He was aware, quoting Isaiah 6, that many people would not be able to hear 'the word' but he must say it anyway.[51] And there was hope that those who did receive the word would respond and bear abundant fruit.

Other examples include the parable of the mustard seed, 'the smallest of all seeds' but which could become 'the greatest of all shrubs'. There are likewise several variations on the sowing, growing and harvest themes spread through the gospels of Matthew, Mark and Luke.

These same ideas are also found in John's gospel, but in a different form. Here 'the seed' and 'the word' are not directly associated with one another, but both ideas are developed in a new and fascinating direction. So, for example, Jesus' words in John directly link the seed falling into the earth with his coming death and resurrection. Here is Jesus' description of his life's work.

*Unless a grain of wheat fall into the ground and die it remains alone, but if it dies it bears much fruit[52].*

................................................

51      Mark 4 v 12

52      John 12 v 24

Likewise 'the word' is powerfully expounded in the prologue to the gospel and it is clear that we are to see this act of Christ as like no ordinary sowing of seed. This one was divine and implicated in the very act of creation.

*In the beginning was the word and the word was with God and the word was God. He was in the beginning with God. All things were made through him and without him was not anything made that was made.*

And it goes on

*And the word became flesh and dwelt among us, full of grace and truth...* [53]

So we see in John that both 'the seed' and 'the word' become all embracing metaphors for the work of Christ and that this work clearly involves the whole creation.

This raises the fascinating possibility that the multiple occurrences of sowing of seed and the resultant harvest in the gospel are not just pictures of a coming Kingdom of Heaven in terms of peace between God and humans, or between

........................................

[53]     The origins of this idea in John Chapter 1 are complex. They certainly lean heavily on the Old Testament idea of 'the word' as in Isaiah, but it has now been personalised, as for example in Proverbs 8, and associated with the very act of creation. The reference in Proverbs speaks of a personified and feminine wisdom of God, who was 'beside God, like a skilled worker' and 'daily his delight' in the process of creation. John's usage probably also draws from a Hebrew tradition which hesitated to speak actually of God and would often use 'The word of God' as a more respectful alternative. Attention should also be paid to the Greek culture of the evangelists day and their use of logos (the greek word translated as 'the word') as more fully meaning 'divine reason'. This may have been part of the reason for making the connection with Proverbs 8.

humans and other humans, but they are also pictures of the coming great Shalom which includes the renewal of the earth and a new harmony among all creatures. This places creation at the very centre of the dream that Jesus sought to live and proclaim, the dream that was couched in terms like 'Good News', 'Kingdom of God', 'Kingdom of Heaven' and 'Peace'. In this case seed sowing and harvest become much more than visual aids, which we should 'spiritualise' away from their original meaning. Instead, the seed is intimately related to the vision. It is about the renewal of creation as pictured by the germination and growth of a seed. Jesus *is* the seed, which *is* the word and the good news has to do with a transformation of the natural world to bring about a great peace. The truth portrayed by this language is also clearly in the mind of other New Testament writers.

## Creation perspectives of Christ in the rest of the New Testament

Take Paul, for instance. Paul's writings are conventionally expounded as the prime locus for understanding the work of Christ. Preachers spend whole sermons on a single verse of Romans! And it is almost always expounded simply in terms of human beings and their relationship with God. Yet for Paul it was bigger than that. There are some verses that simply don't make sense to the human-centred gospel, like the idea, for example, that 'the gospel has been preached to every creature under heaven'[54]. Where does that come from? Search a little further and we notice that Paul's idea of the great reconciliation, the great peace accomplished by Christ actually includes 'all things', which, in the original language, meant everything in the whole creation.

........................................................

54      Colossians 1 v 23

*For in him all the fullness of God was pleased to dwell and through him to reconcile to himself all things, whether on earth or in heaven, making peace by the blood of his cross*[55]

Similar thoughts apply to Jesus resurrection. Tom Wright has recently given the church an extraordinary body of work about the resurrection.[56] We have been used to debating the resurrection over against the scientific laws of this world, but Tom Wright would invite us to see it as a sign of the future. It is the first sign of the breaking in of a whole new creation. He says

*'The resurrection of Jesus offers itself... not as a very odd event within the world as it is, but as the utterly character-istic, prototypical and foundational event within the world as it has begun to be. ... The claim advanced by Christianity is... that with Jesus of Nazareth there is not simply a new religious possibility, nor simply a new ethic, or a new way of salvation, but a new creation.'*[57]

It may be worth stopping for a moment to try to grasp this. If it is right, then the resurrection of Jesus was the beginning of something new in earth history. It was a sign of a new creation that was already breaking into the world and which one day will come in all its fullness.

It also has implications for what we believe about the Holy Spirit which the believers were to receive. If Christ's resurrection was the first sign of the new creation breaking in on the world, then the coming of the Spirit must be to continue that work. And it puts much of the teaching about the Spirit in a new light.

........................................

55     Colossians 1 v 20

56     NT Wright, *The resurrection of the Son of God.* SPCK 2005

57     Tom Wright, *Surprised by hope* SPCK 2007

Take the phrase 'born again' for instance. 'Born again' in some churches has become a shibboleth, a word that defines whether you are in or out, but otherwise almost devoid of meaning or broader connection. I think that the true meaning of born again is intimately related to the renewal of the whole earth.

In 1 Peter we read

*But you have been born anew, not of perishable seed, but of imperishable, through the living and abiding word of God for 'All flesh is grass and all its glory like the flower of the grass. The grass withers and the flower falls, but the word of the Lord abides for ever' That word is the good news which was preached to you.* [58]

Hereagain we have the metaphor of seed sown, explicitly linked to Isaiah 40, but now connected to the idea of being born again. Could it be that the true meaning of being born again in the minds of these first evangelists actually had something to do with the renewal of the earth? Was it, for example, that the Christians were experiencing within themselves a transformation of nature that would ultimately work itself out in the whole creation? Is this born again? Paul makes it very clear that he sees the work of the Spirit within us in terms of a new creation[59] and that the believers were called to live the dream that they had received through Christ out of the power which the Sprit was inspiring within them. So that's it then. The Christians were experiencing the new creation life within them through the Spirit.

........................................

58      1 Peter 1 v 23-25

59      2 Cor 5 v 17

This may be why Paul works with words like 'flesh' in contrast to 'spirit'[60]. He understood that something concerning creation renewal was going on within Christians that could, and should, change their lives for the better. Their lives were to be a sign of the new life that was coming upon the world. This was what it would mean to live in the power of the Spirit. This spirit-filled life would surely affect their behaviour toward one another, but it would also have clear connection with the renewal of creation. This association with creation becomes crystal clear in Romans 8, where Paul says

*The creation waits with eager longing for the revealing of the children of God; For the creation was subjected to futility not of its own will but by the will of him who subjected it in hope; because the creation itself will be set free from its bondage to decay and obtain the glorious liberty of the children of God. We know that the whole creation has been groaning in travail together until now; and not only the creation, but we ourselves, who have the first fruits of the spirit groan inwardly as we wait for adoption...[61]*

So there it is. Paul understood that those who believed should be in the forefront of those who were working for the renewal of creation, for the bringing in of the great dream. The creation was actually waiting for them to take on this responsibility.

This vision of Christ's work applied through the whole of life, even to death. Paul, for example, certainly took up the metaphor of the seed sown when considering the deaths of the first Christians. In this passage, Paul is discussing how they are to think of those who have already died, or in his terms, have 'fallen asleep' and he is at pains to reassure his readers...

..................................................

60      See Romans Chapters 6- 8 for example

61      Romans 8 v 19- 23

*What you sow does not come to life unless it dies. And what you sow is not the body which is to be, but a bare kernel, perhaps of wheat or some other grain. But God gives it a body as he has chosen, and to each kind of seed its own body. For not all flesh is alike...*[62]

There it is again. The very same picture from Isaiah 40, a seed falling into the ground, understood as following from Christ as the divine seed, the one who goes before us all. The death of the believer is now described in terms of a resurrection modelled on Christ's resurrection and part of the renewal of creation. So it is that the New Testament conceives both the life and the death of the believer in terms of the great transformation of creation. Such transformation is, in turn, the promised fulfilment of the dream whose origins we have traced right through the many centuries of biblical writing.

Let me just recap a little now and try to summarise where I think we are up to with the argument. There are three key ideas that I am proposing in this book:

1. A dream arose from the earliest times of biblical history. It arose out of faith in God and was intimately associated with that faith. This dream was about people living, not only at peace with God and with each other, but also at peace with the whole creation. This dream can be expressed in six themes; rest, harmony, fruitfulness, celebration, trust and peace.

2. The realisation of this dream was what Jesus understood to be the good news. He saw himself as announcing the coming of this great peace, which was breaking in on the world. His engagement with the natural world in his words and deeds was more than a metaphor for spiritual

..................................................

62      I Cor 15 v 36

realities. It was indicating that his goal was the renewal of creation itself.

3. The first Christians understood Jesus' achievement to concern the whole creation. The resurrection was a sign of the new creation life, which even then was being made real by the power of the Spirit of Christ within them. They were called to continue Christ's work by living and proclaiming the dream.

For many Christians to embrace such a perspective would be a 'paradigm shift'. And some will find it hard to get their head and heart around these ideas. The work of Christ has to be conceived, not in terms of a human-oriented gospel, but in terms of a whole creation view. It means in practice that environmental concerns cannot be treated as another bolt-on, extra concern that churches might feel obliged to get involved in, but rather that it is genuinely at the core of the good news. We are called to work for this dream. We are empowered by the Spirit to live and proclaim this dream. The environment has to become an issue of discipleship. The days are coming when we shall no longer be able to call ourselves Christians and live an earth-abusive lifestyle. It is time to consider our call.

## Chapter Six
# Considering the call

I would like to begin this chapter with a question. In the UK, and indeed across many parts of the world, we have recently experienced an extraordinary change in public conscious-ness. Environmental issues have suddenly risen to the top of the public agenda. From global news about climate change and peak oil, through to a new interest in wildlife and nature, we have all become considerably more aware of our impact on the earth and its creatures. And the question I would like to pose is 'Is this a movement of the Spirit of God?'

I don't know how you will respond to that. Many people in churches might automatically think in terms of church growth or conversions when they think of the work of the Spirit. However, as was pointed out in Chapter Three, the people of the Bible believed in a God who was at work in the wider world beyond the community of believers. So a movement of the Spirit of God does not have to be confined to the churches. An analogy might make this clear.

Two hundred years ago England was facing a major challenge from a group of people who believed that slave trading was wrong. They worked with tireless energy. And the public consciousness began to change. This was not a minor scuffle. The whole economy appeared to be threatened. Many people with vested interests tried to subvert or oppose the changes that were proposed, including some in the church. It may have looked very messy at the time but from this standpoint two hundred years later I suspect that many believers would agree that the movement to abolish the slave trade was a work of the Spirit of God.

There are some remarkable parallels between today's environmental crisis and the abolition of the slave trade. For example

- The whole economy seemed threatened
- Powerful vested interests opposed the movement
- A new compassion was dawning
- In keeping with the dream of the gospel
- With a renewed sense of right and wrong

Can you see the parallels between the two movements? Some today sense a conflict between necessary environmental action and the economy. Some are denying environmental concerns as hard as they can and opposing every step in response to it. But a new compassion is dawning. I believe that one of the true signature marks of a work of the Spirit in any age is the development of an enlarged compassion in keeping with the biblical dream. We look back now and we can see clearly that slavery was wrong. In those days it was nothing like as obvious and what settled it incontrovertibly was the rising of a compassion which translated into slave people being thought of as fully human.

The biblical word for such a change of mind is repentance. You could say that our whole society has repented of the slave trade. We have changed the way we think. No one today would justify the slave trade. In an earlier chapter, I pointed out how Joanna Macy has described the challenge today in terms of a 'Great Turning' involving the development of a new compassion toward the earth and its creatures. This is similar repentance language.

Another sign of the Spirit concerns moral sensitivity. Such movements always provoke a sea change in morality. We can imagine in the time of the abolition how many people suddenly became nervous of their ill-gotten gains, actively rewrote their histories and became careful about their language. So it is in our society today that things which formerly seemed innocent suddenly take on a new seriousness. That flight to Australia suddenly needs justifying. The daily commute is something to worry about. Plastic bags assume a whole new tone. We worry about polar bears. Jesus taught that the Spirit would convict the world of sin. Are these things the Spirit's work? You must judge.

If there is this great work of God going on among us, how should we respond? The task of the human being as co-creator is to discern the work of the Spirit of God in the world and then to commit our energy to the fulfilment of that work.

When Jesus walked the shores of Galilee and called those first disciples to follow him he was calling them to pursue a dream of the world as it should be. We have seen how this dream involved the renewal of creation, but it also had to be addressed to the social and political realities of Jesus' own day. It is clear that much of Jesus' life and many of his sayings reflect the Roman occupation[63][64]. It may be for this reason that Jesus' favourite descriptions of the world-as-it-should-be were about 'kingdom'. After all it was a political challenge that they were facing. Today we address our own struggle, principally focussed around the threat of human-induced environmental devastation, the question arises as to which descriptive terms are most appropriate to us. How we can express the dream of the-world-as-it-should-be in the culture of our day?

In previous chapters I have shown how different words are used in the Bible for this same dream. It may be that while the political context of Jesus' day demanded he primarily use 'kingdom' metaphors, the environmental challenges of today would encourage us to work primarily with 'Shalom', or the peace which embraces all creation. Both phrases are attempts to express the same reality, which concerns, not just people making peace with God, not just people making peace with each other, but a vision for the peace of all creation. Let's explore the implication of this for the lives of those who would be followers of Jesus today. What is he calling us to? What does it look like to live and proclaim the good news in this society?

It may be that any authentic Christian calling contains three elements:

1. Change the way you see the world
2. Live the new way
3. Proclaim the new way

.................................................

63     Ched Myers – *Binding the Strong Man – a political reading of Mark's story of Jesus* Orbis 2000,

64     Tom Wright – *Jesus and the Victory of God* SPCK 1996

The last four chapters of this book are going to try to flesh these out. As we set out I want to warn that this path is not easy. In Jesus' day there were many who did not choose to follow. There were many, even of the religious, who opposed the young movement. So it will be today. There is a battle going on, as they say, for 'hearts and minds' here. There are deep corruptions in our minds that prevent us even seeing this problem for what it is. There are deep corruptions in our wills that prevent us acting in response. In this chapter and the next I am going to review two mighty obstacles to following Jesus in this generation. The first concerns our economic system and the second some aspects of church teaching.

Some people from North America were visiting a group of indigenous Ecuadorian people and surveying the devastations of logging in their country. The stories were told and the visitors were shocked at the ravaged landscape they encountered. Eventually the Ecuadorian people said to their visitors, 'You have to change the dream of the North'. It was a telling phrase and it spawned one of the most powerful environmental movements in the UK and US today. As a result of this encounter 'Be the Change' runs a national conference in the UK each year for hundreds of people and day seminars up and down this country entitled 'Change the Dream'. The task is immense. The Ecuadorian people see that us people of the industrialised world are currently living in a sort of trance, no longer quite aware of the real world, going through the motions of our lives and destroying the earth in the process. I wonder if you recognise that description. It brings us face to face with capitalism.

I remember, as a young man, going back to my school to help them at a day conference. Old boys had been invited to help facilitate discussions about politics and the economy. These were the early 70s and Keith Joseph was the keynote speaker.

He was a coup for the school and everyone was on best behaviour. He gave us the talk of the day which was to compare a 'command' economy with a 'free' economy, as if these were the only two options, and to tell us along the way that we needed to nurture self-interest if we were to have a free society. I was a keen young Christian at the time and not very well educated in these things, but it was one of those days when I found myself getting to my feet and nervously saying, 'Another word for self-interest is greed' and asking something like 'How does this fit with the teachings of Jesus.' Keith Joseph muttered something about the parable of the talents and the session closed. I was slightly embarrassed and unnerved when, on his way out he signalled to me, to join him. 'Did you really believe that?', he said as we walked along, 'Or were you just making a point?' 'I believe it', I replied. It was the end of that conversation, but it was one of those formative moments for me, the beginning of a life's search for a better way.

Climate change, peak oil, the rise in global population and our general impact on the earth has made it abundantly clear that the capitalist economic model that we are using is fatally flawed, and that one aspect of our calling today is to find a new way to describe economic activity and wealth. Since the days of Adam Smith, and particularly since the neo-liberal reforms of Margaret Thatcher and Ronald Regan, our economic model of life has been seen as the one thing that really cannot be questioned. I believe the system has had its day. We need a new big picture.

The old model of economics can be summarised in terms of one principle and three primary values.

**The old way of thinking**

**Principle – the one thing that the world must pay attention to is market exchange.** Wealth for all will follow from getting this right.

**Primary values** – there are three and they are

Money
Property
Self-interest

This viewpoint insists that money must be held and managed effectively, that property rights must be established in law and that self-interest must be acknowledged as the primary economic driver.

Our business world takes these things as given and non-negotiable. Its echoes can be heard everywhere in a society like ours which sees everything as a commodity and people as consumers. Yet we are reaching the limits of capacity of the earth. We can no longer treat it as an inexhaustible resource and an infinite sink. The prospect of relieving poverty in the Southern hemisphere through simple market mechanisms has become quite incredible in the face of climate change. Likewise the need to respond to global energy security concerns in a more imaginative way is becoming more evident by the day.

October 2008 will be remembered in the annals of economic history for a global financial crisis that shook almost every country in the world. The financial markets came face to face with the fact that they had printed masses of money on the back of highly leveraged credit derivatives that had effectively hidden risk from public accountability. National governments have now bailed out the banks and have promised greater regulation. Meanwhile the shock waves threaten serious global recession. This crash might have been inevitable in the face of a financial system that has escaped political and moral control. Jonathan Porritt said in his opening address to the Schumacher lectures 2008 that he believed this financial crisis heralded the end of the current model of capitalism. It may be that we are about to embark on something new in world economics. We certainly need a new way. This is what it could look like.

## The new way of thinking

**Principle – we need to pay attention to the interconnected systems of the earth that sustain all life**

**Primary Values** – there are three essential ingredients to this

Energy is set to become the primary concern of human society. Already we are seeing carbon trading systems being put into place with the potential for carbon and money to become a dual economy. In the future, as energy becomes more and more precious in itself, we will be calculating the energy cost, as well as the carbon emissions cost, embodied in all of our goods. Oil prices rose to over $150 per barrel in 2008 and then fell back as global recession set in. This price rise may have been the first sign of peak oil being approached. Many reckon that the age of cheap oil is over[65]. As a result we see the major powers in the earth positioning themselves around securing their future energy, while the more prophetic organisations are advocating 'powering down' and building resilient local economies.

At the same time a new reality must dawn about the earth's resources being held in common. Oil and minerals are not there for us to claim, dig up and sell. We must take responsibility for managing these vital resources through a perspective that insists on common ownership, at least for these exhaustible and potentially destructive goods that are laid down in the earth. Likewise there is a sense in which we must manage the physical landscape aware of the impact of our actions on others and on future generations. The rainforests are the most obvious example, but climate change is pointing to the impact of all our behaviours on other common goods, like water supplies. There simply is no alternative but to develop a new sense of commonality.

Finally, it is clear that we must think again about human well-being. Evidence is accumulating that our current lifestyles are making us deeply unhappy and corrupting us so that we are weak and unable to respond to this hour of need.

The essential point about these two ways of thinking is that they are not reconcilable in a simple way. They cannot be simply cobbled together. People have tried to do this. In a seminal book from 1990 Daly and Cobb described how one might draw up an Index for Sustainable Economic Welfare which factored in many of the environmental constraints I have alluded to. A more recent attempt to do this is the 'Five Capitals' approach of Forum for the Future. To my mind the

..................................................

65      For an up to the minute analysis of oil availability and global economy go to www.theoildrum.com

issue that we must face is that the primary values at the heart of capitalism are at odds with aspects of the necessary vision for our future. There really is a deep level conflict over property rights, self-interest and trying to reduce everything to money value. This is manifested by business and political interests, who will make noises about environmental concerns, but will fail to do certain necessary things because they conflict with market interests.

This is not to imply that market mechanisms are not important in coordinating complex systems of exchange and as a means of harnessing new technologies and allowing their efficient application. It is rather to place a new paradigm over and beyond the originating market paradigm, a bit like Einstein's relativity came to superimpose itself on Newtonian mechanics, not by denying the realities on which it was based, but by setting a much bigger frame of reference and allowing the definition of some areas where the simple, originating 'laws' did not apply. So in practice we need to set ourselves to the task of understanding and working with the earth's systems. Within that we shall, in certain areas, use market mechanisms to ensure efficient cooperative behaviour. In other words there is a clear hierarchy of ideas to be established. The future is not the simple capitalism that we have known.

To put all this in a biblical frame is surprisingly easy and surprisingly hard. It is easy because the teaching is all there. It is hard because we have half known this stuff for years and have become dull to its challenge. The key texts have to do with Mammon. Mammon is now an archaic word, but it was used in the New Testament to symbolise the link between money and greed. Mammon was presented as a 'person' opposed to God. I invite you to read these words slowly several times and pray that God will make them alive to you.

*No one can serve two masters; for either he will hate the one and love the other or he will be devoted to the one and despise the other. You cannot serve God and mammon.*

How did that feel? For many of us this saying has died the death of a thousand qualifications. Indeed our failure to appreciate the power of it can be traced to the time of the Reformation as business interests joined hands with the new Protestant leaders and together they gradually overcame constraints to usury and unbridled self-interest[66]. Nevertheless, taken at face value, these words challenge capitalism to its roots. The service of 'mammon' *is* actually to place money, property and self-interest as the primary values of a society. What we are experiencing now is the corruption of a society and the people within it due to our worship of mammon.

Jesus expounded this idea more fully in the parable about the rich person in Luke's gospel where he warned, 'beware of all covetousness; for someone's life does not consist in the abundance of possessions.' He told the story about a person, who became rich through many good harvests and built great barns, and then died to the words, 'You fool, tonight your soul is required of you'.[67] There could be no clearer statement against our current economic model.

It may surprise some to notice that this story is probably Jesus own reflection of a similar story in the wild and profoundly sceptical book of Ecclesiastes. There 'the Teacher' tells a story of a rich man who amassed great riches. It has

......................................................

66      RH Tawney Religion and the rise of Capitalism 1926

67      This passage is found in Luke's gospel just prior to the paragraph about 'not being anxious about your life' and 'considering the lilies of the field'. In Matthew this set of sayings is preceded by 'You cannot serve God and mammon'. It is legitimate to wonder whether these sayings and the story were originally part of the same teaching.

precisely the same themes. The writer takes us to the point of the rich person's death and shows us how stupid it all seems from that perspective. With a 'so what was all that about' feel to the prose, the Teacher considers all the worry and work that went into accruing all those riches, expresses concern over who will inherit, and whether they will fritter them away, and concludes that the whole business was quite meaningless. The absurdity of life viewed from the point of death is also a common resource for our more recent existentialist philosophers, like Sartre. And Jesus uses it in this teaching. We tend to push death aside, blindly assuming that our life's projects will live on and ignoring their terrible fragility in the face of our mortality. What, of what we do, will live on? What will there be to show for our lives when we are gone? For Sartre and other existentialists of recent days, this was the great test of meaning and futility. Those who had not faced their death could not live an authentic life. I guess we need to go there.

Yet this rich man's story feels very different when Jesus tells it. I wonder why? One key difference is that the writer of Ecclesiastes had no big story about life, or at least he did not show that in his writings. There are simply no big reference stories in the book. This is a primary reason why he felt forced to conclude the meaninglessness of life. He had no story to live for. By contrast, Jesus' tale of the rich man was placed in the context of a story about the coming of the world-as-it-should-be. And that dream included social justice. This theme is particularly strong in Luke's gospel. It is in Luke, for example , and Luke alone, that we have Mary's song exalting the one who would 'cast down the mighty from their thrones and lift up the humble and lowly'[68]. It is in Luke that Jesus introduces his ministry with those words from Isaiah about setting at liberty those who are oppressed and proclaiming

..................................................

68     Luke 1 v 52

the great Jubilee when slaves would be released and lands returned[69]. In Luke's gospel the beatitudes are rendered so as to include woes to the rich as well as blessings to the poor[70]. Here also we have the compassion of the good Samaritan[71] and the dire warning to the rich man at whose gate Lazarus lay.[72] Luke's gospel leaves us in no doubt that the world-as-it-should-be included a radical enactment of social justice. In fact, this is so strongly stated that is it bordering on the revolutionary. Of course, all this is easy to say, much harder to live.

The environmental movement of the twenty first century is going to ask powerful questions about social justice. Are we, for example, going to turn agricultural land over to growing biofuels to run our cars, forcing grain prices to increase and provoking starvation and political unrest in the poorest countries? World food prices increased substantially through 2007/8 and biofuels are one of several causes. In 2008 we witnessed food riots in over thirty countries.

More complex is the issue of climate change. Here we have the industrialised societies making an impact on the earth way beyond any per capita allocation that might be just. Schemes like 'contraction and convergence' are being mooted, but precious little effective action is being taken. Climate change is no respecter of wealth, and countries such as the US and Australia are already feeling its impact, but there is little doubt that, as usual, it will be the poorest countries who suffer most. They have least resources with which to finance adaptation, their lands may be only marginally fertile, they

....................................................

69      Luke 4 v 16ff

70      Luke 6 v 20ff

71      Luke 10 v 25ff

72      Luke 16 v 19ff

may be most prone to rises in sea level, and they have least clout with others in negotiation. Climate change raises issues of international justice greater than the world has ever seen before.

We need to face these issues squarely. But to do so we need vision. The call to social justice can all too easily appear as a guilt trip. This is where the dream comes in. The dream that has been described in this book is a wholly positive vision for people and creation living in harmony. The themes of rest, harmony, fruitfulness, celebration, trust and peace are things that can be embraced by everyone. Dream is what is missing from our present culture and we sorely need it. As we consider our call, I believe that part of it has to be proclaiming the dream so that people get it, deep down and it becomes part of them.

Words can be cheap though, and integrity comes much harder. Living the dream is a whole new ball game for most of us. At the heart of it is a struggle of will. We simply do not like to restrain ourselves. In our choice-oriented society we have little expectation, or hope, that we might be able to place limits around our own behaviour. This was illustrated recently at a big forum event with a learned panel. In the middle of some quite complex questions about climate change and our behaviour, a lady got up and simply asked, 'So when is the government going to do something to stop me driving my BMW?' In that question lies the problem. In many ways we are an infantile society. We fail to take personal responsibility for our behaviour. The government must make me. Or someone must make me, but I can't change myself.

The upshot of all this is that repentance is complex. It is about changing the way that we think. But it is more than that. It is also about our wills. We need vision and we need behaviour change. We must live this stuff.

The environmental challenge that we face can only be solved by an unprecedented degree of cooperation across the world.

- It needs a working together at an international level on a scale never yet achieved by human beings.
- It requires national governments to act more bravely and radically than they are currently used to.
- It calls on local authorities to raise their game dramatically
- It forces attention on the lives of individuals and the considerable lifestyle changes that are demanded of all of us.

Can we possibly do this? It is not at all obvious we can. If ever there was a time when we should call out to God for help, surely this is it.

## Chapter Seven

# Hacking through the undergrowth

In this chapter I need to delve into a few gritty issues that Christians, in particular, may face in trying to come to terms with all this. If these things don't scratch where it itches for you, skipping this chapter will not affect your appreciation of the rest of the book.

The problem that needs addressing is summed up for me by the perennial questioner who says, after a talk about the environmental challenge and our calling to live the dream, 'I thought our calling was to make new Christians?' This question actually reveals a big mismatch between the sort of thing that I am saying and the 'gospel' as understood by some branches of the church. My immediate response to the question is to point out that Jesus taught us to make 'disciples', but here I would like to unpack this issue in a little more depth than I can in seminars.

The problem lies in a whole bundle of issues associated with heaven, salvation, the gospel, the end times and the duties of

Christians. Much of the church has become focussed on what is called the afterlife. Of course every religion rightly has views about the afterlife. They are vital for comforting the bereaved and for giving us a hope that can withstand the struggles of this world. Yet if a religion becomes primarily focussed on a life after this one, then it can lose touch with any real interest or concern for the present.

The sort of faith I am talking about goes like this:

- The primary concern of Christianity is to ensure that we attain salvation, which means that we are assured of a place in heaven when we die.

- The primary duty of a Christian is to witness to Christ such that others come to believe and are saved, which means attain to an assured place in heaven.

- We involve ourselves in various caring initiatives on the earth simply to witness to the love of God and thereby win people to faith. The earth and human culture are of no lasting significance.

I know how important this is to many people and hesitate even to tread onto this territory, but I sense that I must address this, because such thinking is currently preventing part of the church from any meaningful engagement with what I see as the greatest issue that human society has ever faced, namely that we are threatening the planet, our future and that of all the other creatures of the earth. I also do not think that this belief does justice to the Bible at several points and is in particular difficulties when it comes to any straightforward reading of the gospels.

It turns out that our minds may have inherited a pattern of thought that is more due to history than the gospel accounts of Jesus life and teaching. If we begin, for example, with the classic duality between heaven and hell, we should note that these words do not appear as dual opposites in the Bible. This polarity is the product of medieval Christendom and of days when the church saw itself as having the 'keys of heaven' and was using this and the countervailing idea of hell as a means of social control. We just inherited this thinking. In fact, as I indicated in Chapter Four, heaven is understood biblically as a focus for the dream of the 'world-as-it-should-be' under God and a longing that this 'world-as-it-should-be' would break into our present existence. The central Christian prayer sums it up

*your kingdom come, your will be done on earth as it is in heaven.*

The Christian is called both to pray this prayer and to live it. In Jesus' mind the 'gospel' was to live and proclaim the dream, the new way of life, the world-as-it should-be, that was breaking in on the world. This dream looked ultimately for a new creation, but this was conceived as a completion, not an obliteration of what was already happening. The work which the disciples were then engaged in would one day be gloriously fulfilled. That was the hope.

Tom Wright, in his recent book, *Surprised by Hope,* has exposed the fundamental error in Christian thinking about heaven. He shows that a proper understanding about the ultimate consummation of God's purposes in the world should be focussed around the transformation of the earth in a new creation, not as in popular imagination, the floating off into a disembodied 'heavenly' existence. He interprets the Bible to say that the earth will be ultimately be transformed, like Jesus body was, into a new physicality. This process will be the fulfilment of the work of Christ that has already begun on earth and the completion of the gospel processes that the people of God have prayed and lived for.

The church has been worried about the 'end times' for many years and there are all sorts of weird and wonderful theories around, that can feel quite bizarre to the outsider. Unfortunately, the truth is that some people defend themselves against involvement in the environmental movement because they believe that God is going to destroy the earth. Some even welcome terrible signs of trouble around the earth as herald of this brighter future. Tom Wright's biblically-based thinking challenges this at its heart. He believes that the earth will not be obliterated but transformed, like Jesus' resurrection body, and that the new earth will be partly continuous with what has gone before. He goes on to propose that much of what people have done that is good and of God will go forward into the new creation. This teaching is fascinating and important

- It says that this earth and all the creation
  is of lasting value to God
- It underlines our calling to work now for the gospel
  dream of a peace that embraces all creation
- It promises that our work here will not be lost

Now, if this is true, then we also need to revisit our calling to work for the gospel. What does this mean? If we take the gospel that Jesus gave us seriously then we cannot think that it is simply about making Christians so that they can go to a completely different, disembodied existence in heaven. What Jesus was concerned about was living and proclaiming the dream and calling others to follow him. He was convinced that the coming of the dream was 'in process' in this world and called people to make sacrifice[73] now in order to help bring about the ultimate enactment of the vision, which would take up all their achievements into a new life on a renewed earth. In our day, this becomes a call to Christians to live out their concern for the earth and its creatures and to strive with all the energy that God inspires for the coming of a peace that embraces all creation.

It is fascinating to consider that when the writer of Matthew's gospel wanted to distil the essence of Jesus' teaching for the opening, post-birth, section of his gospel he chose the words of the Sermon on the Mount. For this gospel writer, these words were what it was all about. It is a pity that few churches today teach the Sermon on the Mount as the heart of the gospel. If we did, we would recognise that Christianity is primarily a discipleship movement, or 'lifestyle' movement as we would say in our current vernacular. In other words it is about a belief that results in a different kind of life being lived.

The Sermon on the Mount teaches that genuine disciples will be known, not just by their words, but by the fruit that their lives bear. Jesus says

*Not everyone who says to me Lord, Lord shall enter the kingdom of heaven, but the one who does the will of my Father who is in heaven. (Matthew 7 v 21)*

These painfully apt words are ignored by sections of today's church. Likewise, the accompanying parable about 'the wise man who built his house on a rock' has been divorced from its original call to live in obedience to Christ and reduced to an

....................................................

73     This is how for example we can understand the call to lay up 'treasure in heaven'. It was to live sacrificially now in bringing in the dream, with a promise that one day this work would be completed as heaven becomes manifest on earth.

essentially meaningless chorus for children. The real message about this wise man story is that the foundations of a true faith are found in action. There really is no escaping the fact that authentic Christianity concerns a belief that leads to a radically different kind of life.

This is underlined by an implicit assumption of the gospels that points to the lasting value of the work that people do here. Jesus shows a clear and abiding concern for the people and society among which he moves. He exhorts the Christians to be as yeast in a loaf of bread, a light to the world, a city on a hill and the salt of the earth. These pictures presume lasting value for the society and call the disciples to get stuck in. When Jesus does speak of the end times, there is a prospect of judgement, there is a discontinuity, but there is also continuity. One of the most beautiful passages in this regard is the Beatitudes. Jesus was aware that people would suffer in various ways for living the life that would transform the world. He wanted them to know that they did not suffer in vain. So the great Sermon includes:

*Blessed are the poor in spirit for theirs is the kingdom of heaven*

*Blessed are the meek for they shall inherit the earth*

*Blessed are those who hunger and thirst for righteousness for they shall be satisfied...*

*Blessed are the peacemakers for they shall be called children of God...*

It is a message of reassurance that what we have done in this world actually matters, that however great the transformation that may occur in the coming of the new creation, those who have laboured in this time, even out of the public gaze, will be honoured for their work. I hope you see from this that the sort of gospel being offered through these texts is rather different from the simplistic one that is only about 'going to' heaven. And that the calling to Christians is very much more than simply witnessing so that people come to faith. We are to live and proclaim the dream and, in our day, in accordance with the great movement of the Spirit, that means paying special attention to the peace that embraces all creation.

There are two primary reasons why we have lost the plot about what Christians are called to do. Firstly, the apostle Paul, in his calling to reach the Gentile world, needed to distance himself from the Jewish law. The struggle to universalise the faith demanded that the Gentiles not be forced to keep the law. Paul's writings were therefore filled with assurances that people were essentially saved by God's grace, and through faith, rather than by the 'works' of the law. This led to a popular distinction being made at that time between those who said they had 'faith' and those who thought the gospel was about what you did, that is, about 'works'. The letter of James dealt with this very question. James was Jesus' brother and had become head of the church in Jerusalem. He was aware that the Jewish law had been fulfilled in Christ and described the 'Royal law' as that which bore on all Christians. This Royal law was the summary of the law that Jesus offered about loving God and loving your neighbour. Yet James was very concerned about the potential split developing in the church between those who saw the faith as something to be 'believed' and those who reckoned that it must be 'lived out'. As a result James tells us categorically that 'faith, by itself, if it has no works, is dead' and goes on to give us one of the sharpest writings on social justice in the New Testament. We need to hear the message of James today. We must live the dream.

This early difficulty of Paul's was compounded in Christian history by Luther. He had a different problem. In his day the church was teaching that people could buy their way into heaven with 'works' of charity to the church. Giving to the church could, for example, secure the saying of masses on behalf of the dead and speed their way to heaven. This corruption, as Luther rightly saw it, had to be confronted and Luther did this by stressing that Christians were saved through faith, not by any 'works'. This was interpreted by some who would follow into a pious form of Christianity whereby there was little that believers actually had to *do* to get to heaven. Luther had helped in one sense to distance the emerging reformed church from the corruption of his day, but his approach had the downside of emphasising a version of the faith that was divorced from the original radical, reforming movement that Jesus began.

So it is that both Paul and Luther came to emphasise faith over against 'works', but in each case they were not contending against the 'works' of a disciple in living out the gospel of Jesus. Paul had to contend against the Jewish law and Luther against the corruption of the church. This historical process has led to Christian traditions which no longer teach the gospel as Jesus gave it to us and deny our calling to seriously engage with living out the dream.

So where does all this leave you? We clearly have deep rooted problems in the society in terms of our economic system and in at least parts of the church in terms of belief. Given the seriousness of our situation today with regard to our relationship with the earth and its creatures, I wonder whether you think we can respond adequately?

I guess the big question that underlies this is 'Do we have the imagination as a species to rise to the challenges that we face?' I have to say, thinking at a mere human level, that I don't know whether we can. But we have this story, this dream, and the One who called us to follow. We have the promise of the Spirit, who can work within us to make it real and galvanise our will.

Dare we set out to turn this dream into reality? If we don't then I guess God might decide, as in Jeremiah's vision, to recast the clay.

Another way of putting the test is to use the parable of the sower and wonder what sort of soil we will prove to be? Can we hear and respond to the word that God brings today? Or will we harden our hearts like the seed that fell on the path, or be choked with the brambles of our selfish anxieties, or act superficially only to be burnt up in the heat of opposition. It remains to be seen. I don't think it is an exaggeration to say that the future of the earth hangs in the balance.

## Chapter Eight

# The dream touches our inner lives

I have a strong sense that we will fail to address the environmental challenges of today if we think that they are a purely instrumental, 'out there' sort of problem that can be dealt with through the mechanics of some changing-your-light-bulbs, carbon reduction programme. I believe that we can only respond well if we examine ourselves deep within, and that means understanding our inner lives. In the next two chapters I mean to explore three different ways that human beings have developed to try to bring our inner lives in touch with the outer world and how these might be important in addressing the environmental challenges that we now face.

### The use of story

All human cultures have found a way of telling stories. There may be nothing more entertaining to a human being than a story well told. They are a rich, multi-faceted resource for reflecting on life and perform all sorts of deep social functions like binding groups together and negotiating beliefs, values and commitments. You may not have thought of it like this before, but the stories that each of us tells about life are like a home base for our minds. They are the way we are making sense of our experience[74]. As we go through life we create something of a big story about ourselves which may include the story of our family, our neighbourhood, our career and our culture. It is an important task. Within the sea of our seething inner motivations and drives there emerges this story, like an anchor, of who we are. We are participants in this family, living among these people, doing this kind of work, for the good of our society. So the traditional story goes. You may have different categories for yours. No matter. None of this is straightforward. As our lives change so our story tries to keep pace with it all. Sometimes we may pass through times of crisis when we can make no sense of things at all, our inner life may feel chaotic, and it may feel like there is nothing worth living for.

...................................................

74      Alastair MacIntyre says for example, 'There is no way to give us understanding of any society, including our own, except through the stock of stories which constitute its initial dramatic resources' *After Virtue* Duckworth 1981, 1985 p216

Such are our stories. They are actually not freely made up, even though it appears that way. Our stories are a reflection, not only of our experience, but also of our beliefs, values and commitments. Stories always betray values. These values may be formed to some degree by those around us and to some degree in tension with these others. So, for example, any culture contains a whole load of fictional stories. Some we will love and some we will despise. And part of our reason for reacting like this is how these fictional stories relate to our values. The conflict of values can be very creative.

The problem for us today is that many conventional reference points for our stories are not as strong as they once were. Families are a shifting reality for many of us. Its members may be spread about the globe and relationships may be fragile. Likewise neighbourhoods have often become weak, particularly in cities, as personal transport makes us all more mobile and invisible to one another. The culture and its institutions are also in flux as the demands of the free market make for radical, ongoing change. Careers are no longer life-long and every job only exists until the next restructure. This has been further compounded by postmodernism, which, as we saw in Chapter One, has deliberately cast doubt over the justifying stories of our institutions and the values of our inherited culture.

The result is that it is hard to have any sense of settled story today. Antony Giddens proposed back in the '80s that what really underlay the rise of counselling was the need to help people form their story in a world that no longer affirmed them naturally.[75] Others have seen our fervent consumerism as an attempt to meet such inner needs.[76]

Another way of seeing this postmodern era is that it reflects a society in transition, where one set of stories no longer quite makes sense and a new story or stories is about to break in on the world. I believe that a new big story, or metanarrative, is already taking shape, emerging like a colossus out of the mess of our chaotic consumerism, and it will be

*the story of how human beings came to live in tune with the earth, or not.*

With 6.7 billion people now impacting the earth, it is clear that we can no longer avoid this story. What I think we will see in the coming decades is that this story will grow in reach and importance so that it feels like it is a primary reference point for the world and the focus for all sorts of political and social innovation. It may even come to be one of the greatest stories in human history. By the end of this century the narrative's building blocks will be in place. We will have experienced many things. Some climate change seems inevitable. That, combined with the challenge to energy resources, is likely to make for social and political struggle across the world, with the poorest peoples suffering most. There will be some species loss and considerable ecological destruction. That much is given, but it is not clear how bad any of these affects will be. It all depends on how we respond. There will be heroes and villains in this story and there will be a mass of people who try to bury their heads in the sand.

................................................

75      Giddens A Modernity and Self-Identity – Self an society in the Late Modern Age Stanford Univ Press 1991

76      James O Affluenza Vermilion 2008

I wonder what part faith might play in this great story that is taking shape around us? Faith communities have not been conspicuous leaders so far. Part of the reason for this might be the way that we tell our stories of faith.

There are many ways of telling the big story of a complex set of narratives like the Bible. Christian interpretation of the Bible story has generally focussed on Adam, as a representative of humanity, and on human disobedience that, in turn, corrupted human society and the whole creation. It then sees Christ as the second Adam who comes to restore all things. This is the great story that is rehearsed every year at Carol Services around the world. Such a telling of the whole Bible story *could* have serious resonance with the challenges we face today as the corruption of human society is all too clearly linked with the abuse of creation. And we might hope in Christ for a change of heart that will allow human beings to lead a process of restoration across the earth. Yet the sad truth is that this story has often been told as relating to human beings only, as concerned primarily with individual disobedience, and as providing an assurance of a life beyond.

In this book I have explored another way of telling the Christian story of the Bible that might complement the traditional interpretation. This begins with a faith that arose in intimate contact with nature and began to articulate a dream for a life that was both at peace with God and with creation. Indeed the two were inextricably linked. Harmony with God would be modelled on the harmony in creation[77]. The fruitfulness of the earth would be a sign of God's blessing on their community. The celebrations of the people would focus on the graciousness of God through the natural world. And they would dream of more. They would dream of a world made

---

77    These themes are explored in Chapter Two

right, so different and so deep that even the animals were at peace with each other. This coming 'Shalom' would become part of the thinking of Jesus of Nazareth and an integral part of the good news that he lived and proclaimed. His death and resurrection would be understood by those who followed as the first sign of the new creation, that was breaking in on the world and the giving of a new inner strength, which the disciples would experience as they sought to transform the world.

This second way of understanding the Christian faith leaves no room for disengagement with nature. It makes no allowance for human-centred views that disregard our creaturehood. And it provides themes to live by, through which we can articulate the hope that is within us, and encourage others to follow in this path. It adds up to a call to consciously embrace our responsibilities as co-creators in the shaping of earth history.

Associated with the big earth story will be all sorts of subsidiary stories, which are also of importance. These are already breaking in on our consciousness. See how wild life stories have assumed a new prominence. In the UK we have experienced the upsurge in popularity of *Springwatch,* a story-based programme that opens our eyes to wildlife around us. It is not always a comforting spectacle. I remember the coffee time conversations on the day after the mother owl had swallowed her chick live on TV! But it is real, and opens our eyes to what is all around us in a way that we urban dwellers often otherwise miss. There can be little doubt that we are becoming aware of the natural world and motivated to care for it through story.

The naturalist Stephen Jay Gould has said

*'We cannot win this battle to save our species and environments without forging an emotional bond between ourselves*

*and nature for we will not fight to save what we do not love[78].'*

Stories help us to feel this problem. Finding and telling wild life and other earth-centred stories is something that many of us could embrace. Constructing this type of story, or even just relaying it, is a strangely powerful experience. It puts us in touch with our own deepest feelings about the natural world and heals something of our own inner disconnect.

## The use of Reason

A second means of dealing with our inner life is to use reason. Reason is about logical deduction, trying to make connections between experiences and pre-existing ideas in such a way as to build reliable knowledge. Reason is a vital component of all good societies and an originator of what we now call science. It is interesting to note that nature was one of the first subjects of reason. People wanted to work out how the world worked. Even monkeys have been shown to work with tools to get their food. To do so, they experiment, try something, learn and pass on their knowledge to their young. Likewise at a cultural level, legal systems are a vital ground for reason in any culture. The simple law code, known as the *Book of the Covenant,* in the book of Exodus[79] offers detailed prescriptions for how people managed their life in an early pastoral society. It is all about sheep and oxen and what should happen when they wander or get ill, or are killed and there is a dispute. The outworking of this law code through a system of judges is a primary example of the ancient use of reason and such law codes are vital to the well-being of any society. We have come to think of faith as somehow in conflict with reason, but history tells a different story. The

...................................................

78      Quote relayed from Antony Nanson, storyteller

79      Exodus 20 - 23

first universities grew from colleges for training priests. And why did they happen? They were an outgrowth of a way of seeing the world that encouraged debate, believed in a world that could be made sense of and a God who revealed things to human beings.

The story of the origins of science is similar. Of course aspects of science have arisen in many cultures. The Greeks held a certain sort of atomic theory. The Chinese invented fireworks. But it may be that truly fruitful scientific investigation is built on a decisive interaction between theory and experiment. That arose just once in human history. And it came out of medieval Christendom. Many scholars now agree that Christian belief was a crucial underpinning of the rise of science[80]. While the institutional church opposed some aspects of the rise of science for its own political ends, the overall way that Christian people understood the world encouraged the development of science. Isaac Newton has always been exalted as a pioneer of science, yet it is little known that he spent almost as much time in study of the Bible as in scientific endeavour. In fact many of the first scientists were active Christians. It seems that the belief that the world was created by a being, who was dependable, and rational, naturally led to the idea that the material world itself might be something that could be understood and investigated. No other society has ever come up with the dynamic between theory and experiment that is at the heart of modern science. And science is set to be one crucial component of the twenty first century. We are going to need all its devices if we are to rise to the challenges that are being presented to us.

................................................

80      See for example Rodney Stark *For the glory of God* Chap 2 Princeton University Press 2002

Yet reason can be overdone and the sort of faith that I have just described can also be inadequate. Let me explain why. Some cultures have tried to exalt reason to such a degree that nothing else counts. The Greeks certainly did this and the writings of Plato and Aristotle and others testify to it. In our modern era the so-called Enlightenment tried to apply scientific reasoning to all aspects of society. This was misguided. Science was good for some things and not others. The attempt to apply science and reason to everything about life is partly responsible for the absence of meaning and purpose in our society today. Science simply cannot give meaning and purpose. That is the province of story, which works in a deliberately holistic fashion, to integrate all that we are, including the inner life of our emotions. Philosophers such as Immanuel Kant taught that true knowledge was always to be found by rising above our 'passions' into the realm of abstract reason. From this lofty vantage point we could see the world as it truly is and so prescribe for society. The issue with this was that it was 'abstract'. The world of ideas was divorced from the reality of life and cut off from the emotions, compassion, kindness and all the other things that go to make up a good society. More than that it is an arrogance to think that we *can* rise to a place where we float around in abstract ideas. In fact, and this has now been powerfully proven by the postmodernists, lots of apparently rational ideas of the Enlightenment period were actually the product of pre-existing commitments that were far from rational[81].

In our present scene this pretend rationalism is exemplified by the climate change sceptics, a tiny band of scientific popularisers, who make their name by confusing the public with pseudo-science. These people purport to use the language of

81      See for example, though its a tough read, Richard Rorty *Philosophy and the mirror of nature* Princeton University Press 1980

reason and evidence, while actually being informed by a whole host of motives that have nothing to do with the evidence. It is necessary for all of us to own our deepest commitments and motivations and to recognise the power they have over our rational and moral pretensions. If we fail to do this we will never respond adequately to the challenges we face.

For the last year or so I have been working on a climate change campaign that encourages people to leave their cars at home one day each week. It's called *Chooseday* and has been great fun to be part of. In the process I have talked to many people about their lifestyle. I try to do it in an open and non-judgemental way, recognising that we are all hopelessly compromised in our present oil-addicted culture and that we must be merciful to each other. Anyway, what I have found is this. Many people begin by saying they are not sure the science is right. They will then quote some sceptical position about the science of climate change as if they have the knowledge to judge these things. Never have so many people acted as if they understood climatology! I don't pretend to understand climatology and I actually did scientific research for ten years. As a scientist I have learnt to respect the knowledge and experience of other scientists. Not so the sceptics. They wade in with their views. Then, as the conversation goes on, it almost always reveals something else. This person's lifestyle is threatened by climate change. There is something they are doing, something in their daily life, whereby believing in climate change would logically require them to change their ways. So they look for a reason to disbelieve. Others in this field have studied this phenomenon and it is now widely accepted that opinions often follow, rather than lead, behaviour. This all fits in with a huge set of data showing that we are not as rational as we think and that our powers of self-justification are immense. Mere information does not do the business in climate change communication. We need other forms of motivation as provided, for example, by story and the moral persuasion that lies within a story.

This critique of science also rebounds on faith, because the pursuit of reason in the totalitarian sort of way that it has been pursued during the Enlightenment does something to the way that people think about God. In such a culture people, who believe in God, tend to conceive God as a creator, who is largely transcendent, that is, abstracted from this world. In simple terms, God is seen as 'up there', beyond and largely separate from the earth and the lives of its creatures. The Creator is understood as having made creation as like an object. In extreme form such an attitude gave rise to a form of belief known as 'Deism', which had little or no place for God's ongoing interaction with this world. The difficulty with this way of thinking comes in that humans, in response, also tend to see the world as an object that they can stand aloof from and from there they assume that it is okay to manipulate the world at will.

This is the heart of the critique of 'stewardship' as embraced by some parts of the church today. Crudely, the idea is that, God, the rightful owner of the earth, has gone away and left it to us to look after as stewards. At one level it sounds OK, but it encourages an attitude that assumes we humans are utterly distinct from the earth. We are no longer creatures. We are stewards of the earth, standing in the place of a distant, transcendent God and similarly abstracted from it.

This way of thinking about God has actually sunk quite deep into the popular mind. I often find myself fielding a question at the end of seminars that goes something like, 'Well God gave us the earth to use, why shouldn't we get on and use it?' I hope that the reader can see through to the horror of this way of thinking for themselves now, but the heart of the problem is probably a theological misunderstanding. You see authentic Christianity actually understands God as both transcendent and *immanent,* that is, present with us now, active in the world and within us in terms of real experience. So God is not just out there presiding, as it were, over creation, God is understood to be here with us, alive and active. This makes a huge difference to the sort of response that human beings might make and brings us to the third way of dealing with our inner life, that of contemplation.

## Chapter Nine
# The contemplative life

Alastair McIntosh has been a powerful activist. He has bravely taken on a whole series of issues about land and power on Scottish Islands and his book *Soil and Soul* has been widely acclaimed. Yet, for all the action, Alastair is convinced that the key to transformational change is the inner life. Much radical politics fails because the people involved have not dealt with their own internal issues. Richard Rohr takes a similar line. He has a Centre for Contemplation and Action, but recognises the need to focus mainly on contemplation.[82] He says, 'I have seen far too many activists who are not the answer. Their head answer is largely right, but the energy, the style and the soul are not.' It seems that, whether we like it or not, our inner lives tend to dictate what we can achieve. A set of ideas is not enough. A consuming energy is not enough. We need an inner wholeness that can come through contemplation.

...................................................

82      Richard Rohr *Everything belongs – the gift of contemplative prayer* 2003 p 74

At the outset of this chapter, I want to own up to being a beginner in contemplation. I would direct the reader to folk like Richard Rohr or John Main for more mature insights. Yet I have sensed the importance of contemplative practice and maybe what follows can act as a signpost to others who are considering this path.

Contemplation can be defined as paying attention. It is about a way of seeing. We live in a world today where we are deluged with information. The emails come in. The mobiles ring. A text here. A website there. Excited by the process, we can all too easily become people who are skimming over the surface of life. John Naish has described our condition as infobesity[83], seeing it as a different sort of fatness and producing profound stress. There is a sense that we need to slow down, to settle and pay attention to things in a new sort of way.

Likewise we need to pay attention to ourselves. Our hyper-stimulated lives can be an excuse for not recognising what is going on within us. We are really complex people. There are things that we acknowledge about ourselves and there are things that we suppress or hide even from our own conscious minds. To become aware of ourselves at a deep level, to acknowledge our 'shadow side', without necessarily following its lead, can be a great healing to the soul and a source of strength. The alternative, say many, is that we project onto others those things about ourselves that we refuse to acknowledge. We demonise others because of our own inner failings. Perhaps this is the deeper meaning in Jesus's saying 'Take the log out of your own eye and then you will see clearly to take the speck out of your neighbour's eye.'[84]

......................................................

83      John Naish *Enough-breaking free from the world of more* 2008
84      Matthew 7 v 5

At various places in this book I have pointed to the need for inner transformation if we are to respond adequately to the environmental crisis that is breaking on the world. There are certain dominant ways of seeing the world that we have inherited from the culture around us that are implicitly abusive of the earth. Our economics, politics and even religion are shot through with arrogant assumptions about human beings as the only creatures on earth really worth considering, with the earth simply as a stage on which the human drama is worked out. This has to change. We need to see ourselves as creatures, albeit extraordinary and frustrated creatures, that are intimately joined into all the complex ecosystems around us. It may be that contemplation is a primary means that we can attain to such a deep change of worldview.

To begin to pay attention we need to cultivate a certain sort of stillness. While my wife and I were on holiday this year, we took a picnic down to some rocks on the beach. Having no agenda and nothing that we had to do, we found ourselves just staring into a rock pool. At first it just presented as a beautiful still picture with reds and greens, plants and cockley, mussel-like things with shells. After a few seconds waiting there, we saw a shrimp, almost invisible, as it moved over the surface of the rock. Then we saw another and another. After another space of time my wife said, 'Look, that shell it is moving.' I looked and sure enough, one of them was moving, very slowly, twisting and turning. As we looked further we began to see that they were all moving, as in some great dance. So it was that the rockpool came alive for us. We saw things we did not even know were there.

So it is, I think, with contemplation. By cultivating a sense of paying attention, to ourselves and, particularly to the natural world, we come to 'see' differently. From such a vantage point we can find freedom from dominant and controlling worldviews and find a settledness and peace from which to live a better life.

For the past thirty years or so my primary resource for faith has been the Judaeo-Christian scriptures. During that time I have progressed in the way that I have read the Bible. Starting off as a zealous young Christian my dominant mode of reading was that of reason. I was trying to formulate doctrine, to get things right, to control and be sure of what I believed. I still do that to some degree and, of course, reason remains an important tool in Bible study, particularly for academic theologians. Later in life I have discovered the Bible as narrative, exploring the rich and diverse stories within the canon. I have tried to enter into the stories, to feel the passion and energies that underline them and the theological, social and political struggles with which people were engaged. As part of that journey I have developed a method of 'Bible telling' to bring the words to bear on public life. Most recently, I have found a new thread within the Bible, which appears to be designed to promote contemplation and which focuses on the natural world.

I want to introduce this contemplative thread to you using the Book of Job. Job is a tough book to read straight through. Thirty seven chapters of an attempt at reason, which goes something like; God has promised to look after those who live righteously. Job is a good man, so why is he suffering? And the argument goes frankly nowhere. Some of his advisors say, 'Well, Job must really have done wrong'. Job says 'No, I have not.' And there is no resolution. Until something happens. In Chapter Thirty Eight the discourse changes. Job is confronted directly by God, who challenges him with powerful images of the natural world.

*Where were you when I laid the foundations of the earth?*
*Tell me if you have understanding...*

*Can you bind the chains of the Pleiades?*
*Or loose the cords of Orion?..*

*Is it by your wisdom that the hawk soars*
*and spreads its wings toward the south?..*

And so it goes on, in a rebuke to Job. But what for? What had he done wrong? Well, nothing in terms of reason. There is no resolution of the great debate, as it were, but there is something new. Job is required to take up a new attitude of mind. He is to be humbled. No longer to complain that God should be micromanaging the world according to his structures of reason, Job is to prostrate himself before the actual presence of God as witnessed to by creation. The call is to a deep relationship with God through creation. Job is being asked to feel himself as creature and to sense the interconnectedness of all things and the reality of the very presence of God in the world. This, I suggest is the heart of contemplation. Job is modelling for us the sort of repentance that we need at the beginning of the twenty first century.

In Chapter two I quoted the dream of the world made right from Micah that concludes with these lines

*But they shall sit everyone under their vine and under their fig tree and none shall make them afraid[85].*

Some say that this sitting under the vine was a practice associated with meditation. People actually did go and sit in stillness under their vine and their fig tree and contemplate life. As an allotment holder I can understand this at a simple level. The idea is very attractive. People like to simply

---

85      Micah 4 v 4

*be* on allotments. It is a healing sort of experience. We only started ours this year and my wife is really keen on me building a hut, so she can just sit there and be with the things that our growing. Yet this scriptural motif comes at the end of a truly big picture vision in Micah that includes swords being beaten into ploughshares in a world of justice and peace. So the 'sitting under the vine' is most likely the call to meditate on the big picture dream of the world as it should be. Peter Craigie in his commentary on this passage[86] says,

*We will only grasp and be grasped by these words if we move from the surface to the vision that they embody. A few persons in our time have caught the vision: Mahatma Gandhi, Martin Luther King and others have grasped the vision of the world as it might be and allowed the vision to penetrate their efforts to change the world as it is.*

Dare we meditate on living in tune with the earth, imagining what that life might be like? There may be no more powerful thing for us to do.

The gospel of John is obviously different from the other gospels, but I wonder if we are aware of what really is different about it? I think the writer of John is offering a resource for contemplation. He presents Jesus and his life to us as something to meditate on. He does not offer a set of ideas or a programme for action. The other gospels do that. Instead John invites us to dwell on this Jesus and particularly on the relationship between Jesus and the natural world. Let me show you how.

The first chapter of John is extraordinary in many ways, but one aspect that may have escaped our notice is the piece about Nathanael. Jesus describes Nathaniel as 'having no guile'. It is a great compliment, implying a high degree of integrity. Then Jesus goes on to say that he saw him when he was 'under the fig tree'. This, as we have seen, implies the place of contemplation. Nathanael is amazed by this statement, and the implication is some sort of supernatural knowing of Nathanael by Jesus through Nathanael's contemplation. Jesus goes on to promise something that every contemplative might hope for. 'Truly, truly I say to you that you shall see heaven opened...[87]' The vision of heaven, the world-as-it-should-be, the place of God, open to our understanding, is perhaps the ultimate goal of Christian meditation. And in this passage, as it is throughout John's gospel, it is linked specifically to an appreciation of Christ. So it goes on '... and the angels of God descending and descending upon the Son of Man.'

I believe this passage sets the scene for the gospel. It is a specific commendation of the contemplative path and similar characteristics are found in several of the passages that follow.

For example, we saw earlier how the conversation with Nicodemus turned around being 'born again' and how this may have indicated a transformation within a person that would make them a sign of the coming renewal of creation. One could also note at this point that the word for 'born again' here can also be translated 'born from above'. So such a person can be understood to have the life of heaven within them, the vision and energy of the world as it should be. This for John is to live life in the spirit.[88]

One characteristic of such transformative spirituality is to help people break out of the dominant worldviews of the prevailing culture. When he meets the woman at the well in John

..................................................

87      John 1 v 51

88      John 3 v 6

4, Jesus is drawn into what was no doubt a very common religious conversation about the right place to worship, but Jesus subverts the woman's perception with the words 'the hour is coming and now is when the true worshippers will worship the Father in spirit and truth... God is spirit and those who worship God must worship in spirit and truth'. In this way Jesus ducks the dominant religious questions and sets forward a quite different vision. Such subversion is a key aim of contemplation.

Commentators like Richard Rohr see a similar purpose behind the story of the healing of the blind man in John chapter 9. As the authorities rehearse the tired religious argument saying 'Who sinned this man or his parents?', Jesus spits on some clay, rubs it in the man's eyes and tells him to go and wash. He comes back seeing. And his healing becomes a sign of the whole new way of seeing the world that Jesus can give. Such new sight is the aim of the contemplative.

There is another important aspect of this teaching. As we go through the gospel we find that time after time, it is the natural world that is presented as the subject for contemplation. As we have seen throughout this book, the dream arises from creation. So when the people are hungry, the bread becomes the occasion for words about 'the bread of life', of which people will eat and never be hungry again. It is the physical death of a man and his rising that is accompanied by words about Jesus as 'the resurrection and the life'. It is the water at the well that provokes the words about drinking water 'that I shall give' and 'never thirsting again'. It is a vine that provokes the deep words 'I am the vine, you are the branches, dwell in me.'

These are mind-blowing pictures and are but a few examples of the particular characteristic of John's gospel, which is to promote that way of being in our minds which is contemplation. It is a meditation on the natural world that confounds our search to capture ideas, and takes us to a different place, a holistic space beyond the reach of analysis and logic, and to the imagination of a dream of a life with God, a whole quality of life, that can be made present now. Furthermore, and vital to the message of the gospel, is that these meditations point to Christ as the very source of creation renewal. He was the one who was to give his life 'like a grain of wheat that falls into the ground and dies'.

Appreciating the culture of the day can reveal the earth-connectedness of this whole process. It is the last day of the great feast of Tabernacles. This was one of the times each year when all the people gathered in Jerusalem. It was a harvest festival and it was celebrated by the making of a temporary home, like a tent, decorated with branches and leaves. [89] The feast was agricultural and at the heart of it were ritual prayers for rainfall in which four species of plant would be waved in each of the four directions, north, south, east and west. In the days of the Temple there was also a special libation ceremony whereby water was drawn from the Pool of Siloam and taken to the outer Temple where thousands of pilgrims would gather. Here there would be singing and dancing with lighted torches, harps, lyres, cymbals and trumpets. The celebration was magnificent. It was said that

*'He who has not seen rejoicing at the Place of Water Drawing has never seen rejoicing in his life.'*

On the last day of this feast, known as the Great Supplication, seven circuits were made with plants being ritually beaten on the ground and there were special prayers for the coming of the Messiah. It was on that day and in this context that we read

........................................................

89      see Nehemiah 8 v 15-18

*On the last day of the feast, the great day, Jesus stood up and proclaimed, 'If anyone thirst, let them come to me and drink. Those who believe in me, as the scripture says, "Out of their hearts shall flow rivers of living water." (John 7 v 37 – 39)*

So we are to picture a massive feast and a praying for rain and the fruitfulness of the ground, a sense of intimate connection with the earth, a great rejoicing and prayers for the Messiah. Then Jesus spoke. The links are so powerful. Here is the Messiah that is going to renew the earth, whose coming is so transformative that the prayer for water becomes a picture of the coming of the Spirit of God.

This picture summarises John's gospel for me. John offers us a picture of Jesus as the source of all creation and the one through whom it was being transformed. He was the one 'through whom all things were made'[90] and he had come to bring life, as experienced *now*, and known as a *quality* of life. It is interesting that the phrase 'eternal life,' that is so common in John, largely replaces the 'kingdom of God' in the other gospels and signifies, not primarily life after death, but a quality of life that was breaking in on the world, which people could enter into.

When environmentalists tell me, as they often do, that they are not sure about God, but they *are* spiritual, I like to enquire what sort of God they are imagining. Understandably, given our history, most imagine God as the transcendent being who presides over the earth and is disconnected from it. Some go on to recognise how such visions can lead to oppressive forms of religion that do seriously bad things to people. I think that critique is right, but, as mentioned previously, authentic Christianity holds that God is both transcendent, that is, above all, and immanent, which means present now

....................................................

90      John 1 v 3 and v10

113

with us and among us. If it is hard to understand how both these things can be true at once, that is because of our weakness in imagining and our captivity to logical truth above all other. To recognise the immanence of God and the more mystical side of our present day experience is to embrace much, I think, of what all sorts of people today value about spirituality. And it is to allow us to experience that sense of interconnectedness of all life that we so desperately need at this time. Contemplation is a primary means through which God can be known in an immanent, with us now, sense.

So, if John's gospel works in the way that I am suggesting that it does, I wonder what we can draw from it in terms of practical implications for our own contemplative path? The broad approach that I would take from the gospel is that we need to find ways of bringing the experience of the natural world in touch with biblical insight and our focus on Christ. That is surely what John's gospel is commending to us. There will be many different methods of doing this and different styles will suit different people, but the principle of bringing meditation on Christ in touch with creation might be a good starting point for contemplative development.

The prize at the end of this process is perhaps the most awesome gift that is given to human beings to experience. It is the sense of coming home. The restlessness of the human soul has been charted by theologians for centuries[91]. Our basic love for nature has been noted by the romantic poets and also by scientists[92]. As the urban believer in our consumerist society draws near again to God through nature, so they find

......................................................

91      Augustine, for example, spoke of the restlessness of the human soul until it finds its rest in God.

92      EO Wilson, for example, has commented on this widespread phenomenon and calls it 'biophilia'

a fulfilment of their most basic longings. The soul comes into peace as it experiences a deep interconnection with nature and a fulfilment as it senses the love of God. The human being has come home. I have tried to express this coming home in a new telling of one of Jesus' most famous parables. It is called the Prodigal Civilisation and it consists of two interwoven stories.

---

Once there was a man who had two sons

*Once there was a God who, over thousands and millions of years, made a great creation, with a whole of host of creatures upon an earth. And there came a time when one of those creatures came to understand themselves to be special in the eyes of God.*

And the younger of them said to his father, Father give me my share of the inheritance that is due to me. And he divided his living between them.

*And the humans said to God give us our inheritance, and they plundered the earth with mines and drills and rigs, sucking out the black treasure, consuming it in their machines and spewing the gas into the sky..*

Not many days later the younger son gathered all that he had and went on a journey to a far country, and there he squandered his inheritance in loose living

*A great economic system arose fuelled by deep level passions, based on conspicuous consumption and using the black treasure. The people travelled everywhere and nowhere. Forests were destroyed. It was party time. The air was filled with (pause) laughter. But the clouds were gathering.*

And when it had all gone, a great famine arose in the land and he began to be in want. So he went and joined himself to one of the citizens of that country, who sent him into his fields to feed the pigs. And he would gladly have ate from pigs trough, but no one gave him anything.

*It was the climate you see. They hadn't thought of that. And once they had, it was too late. The animals and plants began just to disappear. The desert spread. The wells grew deeper. Water. (pause) Anxious people. (pause) Angry people. (pause) Violent people. The rich built castles. The poor made battering rams.*

And then he realised, he said, Why even my father's hired servants have bread enough to spare but I perish here with hunger. I will arise and go to my Father and say, 'Father I have done wrong against heaven and against you. I am no longer worthy to be called your son, treat me as one of your hired servants. '

*And a few began to dream of a home, they saw a vision of God surrounded by the creatures of the earth, they dreamt of living at peace with God and the creation and they set out to make that real.*

And he arose and set out for his father. And when he was far off his father saw him and had compassion and ran and embraced him.

*And I will leave you to fill in the rest of the story.*

Finally, in this chapter on the inner life, I want to make connection with one other great theme that flows out of the vision of John's gospel, without which such talk of home and fulfilment would be lacking, and that concerns relationships with others. Loneliness is now endemic in the Western world. Retail therapy does not meet our need for friendship. The comfort of the familiar brand does not scratch where it itches. We need to hear again the call to community. The human being is a social animal. We are truly individuals-in-relationship and need to respect both individual and relational poles of our being. The pursuit of reason, as we have seen, is too often dispassionate, and thereby dangerous, and capable of espousing a logic that destroys. We need compassion and the first place that we will exercise compassion is with those around us. So it is that John's gospel focuses in on one primary commandment, to love one another.[93] I believe that learning to live more in tune with the earth is necessarily going to bring us back in touch with one another. A new localism must dawn as travel becomes more precious and a new communal spirit of cooperation will allow for new enterprises. At the heart of this, I suggest, is precisely this gospel dream that to love one another is to experience God.

........................................

93 John 13 v 34, John 15 v 12, John 17 v 21, 26

## Chapter Ten
# Acting it out

There is no expert who is going to solve this for us. There is no techno-fix just round the corner. Our institutions are tired and have been found wanting. Many of our people are listless and can think no further than their own concerns. Yet there are others who are hearing the call. Some recognise the voice of God in it and some do not, but they are united in feeling that immense change is coming. Already there is a certain mourning in the air, for the great animals that are leaving us for ever, for the ice caps and glaciers that are melting and for the world's people about to suffer social unrest and suffering on an unprecedented scale. Now is the time to act. It is now or never. But what shall we do?

It seems to me that we need to associate. Those who feel these things and are willing to commit to action must get together. Human ingenuity is immense, but we need to rethink many aspects of our lives at once, to break down the artificial barriers in our minds that our culture has erected, and cross new thresholds of creativity and practical co-operation.

New communities will arise at this time, of that there is no doubt. EarthAbbey is one such community whose aim is simply to encourage one another to live more in tune with the earth. Creative genius is not well nurtured by rules, so this community will have the lightest touch in terms of constraints and be formed to be self-organising, creating space for people to associate with one another, tell their stories, reflect on their lives and find courage to live the dream.

One of the great gifts of faith to a wider society is the provision of space with which to reflect. There is a profound need today to stop what we are doing and be still, to reflect on ourselves as people and our treatment of the earth. Let the followers of Christ lift their heads and find inspiration, look again to the heavens and envisage the throne of God, look around with compassion and embrace the people and all that lives upon the earth. And let us create space where all sorts of people can join hands, find peace, confront their own inner lives and find inspiration to act well in the world.

The environmental challenges that we face today are so many and so difficult that there is a real danger that we shall be overwhelmed. Our concern could kill us. We could all too easily become deeply depressed and paralysed in terms of creativity. That is why I think the dream is so important. It is a message of hope and a vision for life. I invite you now to consider how you might apply the themes of that dream into your situation.

# Rest

It seems strange to begin an agenda for changing the world with the idea of rest, but I think it may be appropriate. Our anxious and busy lives may be preventing us ever really facing the truth about ourselves. Perhaps first of all we simply need to learn to be still. There is so much environmental busyness around. Everyone has their own set of programmes, their own projects and brands that they are protecting and nurturing. Perhaps it is time to stop and take stock. I remember that Gandhi would spend two hours a day spinning. But he was not ineffective. I have never quite known what to do with Jesus' words when he said, 'Come to me all who labour and are heavy laden and I will give your rest.' It sounds really nice. They are the sort of words that give you a nice feeling, and then are lost in the pressures of the day. I wonder what it would mean to actually discover the truth of them.

The church is tired and looking for help, often in the wrong direction. Those who follow the teacher from Nazareth need to share their insights and rediscover the radical lifestyle movement that was the original Christianity. Those who contribute to the future will be those who are trying to live the future. As we offer our lives afresh to God to serve the gospel which looks for the peace of all creation, then we need to cash this in terms of re-imagined lives, breaking out of the constraints of our current culture and worldview. We need to make real those words in Romans 12 v 1

*I appeal to you therefore brothers and sisters, to present your bodies as a living sacrifice, holy and acceptable to God, which is your spiritual worship. Do not be conformed to this world but be transformed by the renewal of your mind, that you may prove what is the will of God, what is good and acceptable and perfect.*

One of the 'mind-forged manacles'[94] that we suffer from concerns work. Even as recently as the 1970s it was common for only one member of a family to be in paid work. Since the dawn of the neo-liberal movement more and more families

94      From Tom Hodgkinson *How to be Free* Chap 1 – taken originally from William Blake Songs of experience

have first wanted, and then felt to need, a double income. Tom Hodgkinson in *'How to be Free'* suggests that we are anxious today because we have been made anxious. He says that we rush around desperately in both work and leisure fruitlessly trying to allay our anxiety, often by shopping. He then asks the unthinkable, like, I mean, *why* do we work so hard? I hear echoes of Ecclesiastes as he points to the meaninglessness of much of our work, and the liberating consequences of realising that. The book is mad in places and I am sure it will annoy many, but there is something very interesting and truly alternative in what he is saying. Part of our bondage today is to paid work. My wife was ill recently. A post-viral thing that went on for several months. To be at home and rest meant that she met some neighbours, enjoyed the allotment and recovered her bounce. It felt like such a good deal that we have both thought of going part-time since! I wonder 'Dare we earn less and work less?' It feels like a tough call, but many others are exploring this path to freedom.

I think also that we may need to help each other to pray at this time. Some of the traditional modes of prayer are tired. The hymns, which form the main focus of devotion in many churches today, largely fail to engage with the issues raised in this book. Many people are rediscovering the inner space created by forms of meditation and multi-sensory prayer. We need all sorts of creative input in this area. It is clear that we need to come to terms with how we see ourselves and the earth at a very deep level if we are going to be ready to change our lives.

# Harmony

The progressive urbanisation of human society has left us dramatically out of touch with the natural world. Our out-of-the-house-into-the-car mentalities leave us in a bubble of anxiety and out of touch with the very God-given resource that can restore our souls. We have to work to reintroduce people to nature. Whether it is by working on an allotment or taking a walk in the wild, our city bound people need help to connect.

Such reconnection has a deep side. It may be that we are going to have to rethink the whole way that we educate ourselves. No longer can we split knowledge into watertight disciplines, pursuing theoretical ideas that fail to engage with each other or with the natural world. Science is a great servant, but a poor master. The farmer who eagerly embraces the latest high yield variant, that incidentally needs enormous quantities of water, fertiliser and pesticide, may feel like they are at the cutting edge of progress, while they sow the seeds of future calamity.[95] The business person who conceives the latest plastic doll that in three years will simply go to landfill, needs to think again. There can be no excuse now for failing to engage in holistic earth-centred thinking. And that needs a new educational model. EarthAbbey is looking to establish an EarthLife Centre dedicated to the study of the earth as a living system and bringing together, science, theology, philosophy and psychology, together with developing the practical crafts associated with permaculture and passive solar housing that we need today. The Centre for Alternative Technology at Machynleth is a world leader in this field of holistic thinking and practice.

Every aspect of our lives will need to be examined against the need to live in harmony with the natural world. Climate change is forcing a complete re-evaluation of our housing strategies. Energy consumption will be minimised by the adaptation of

---

95      Colin Tudge *So shall we reap* 2001 carefully charts the dangers of scientific arrogance in the field of agriculture.

houses. New build may offer vision, but will not deal with the bulk of the housing stock, which must be renewed by adaptation. A whole new set of energy mitigation technologies and trades will arise. George Marshall is not formally trained in architecture and design, but set himself to understand and refit his own terrace house in Oxford so as to make it more efficient and earth friendly. His website, the yellow house[96], reports his calculations and adaptations regarding heating, the building of a sun room to capture passive solar energy, the need for high thermal mass materials, even the reuse of bath water in the loo. His practical ingenuity has recently been published in a how to book by Hamlyn entitled *Carbon Detox: Your step-by-step guide to getting real about climate change* which sets out to cover a whole range of carbon reduction behaviour, as well as exposing some of the 'greenwash' that we are all suffering from.

Charting an harmonious path into the future also needs good thinking. The recent biofuels fiasco proved our potential for foolish, ill-thought out measures. In 2050 the earth may have 10 billion people on it. All the issues of today will be magnified. Even feeding people will be a major challenge. Climate change has proved the need to listen hard to the scientific constraints within which we live. Evidence-based thinking and conversation is a vital component of the future as we continue to discover the intricacies and vulnerabilities of our ecosystems. Some environmentalists seem to have declared open season on knowledge. There are some amazing and whacky theories used to support practical initiatives that appear to have little evidential basis. We must develop a proper rigour concerning areas where scientific thinking can help us, but we must consider this within a much bigger holistic paradigm that speaks about purpose and meaning in our relationship

96     http://www.theyellowhouse.org.uk

with the earth. Such a paradigm can only arise from philoso-phers, theologians and other big picture thinkers.

# Fruitfulness

Harmonious living goes together with fruitfulness. Paying attention to nature will naturally foster a desire to grow food. This will be enhanced by the threat of social unrest and eco-nomic hardship as horticulture is perceived to be a viable form of local resilience. Spaces in towns and cities will become prized for their horticultural potential and people will learn how to grow food on sustainable principles.

One of the primary carriers of this vision today is the Permaculture movement. Permaculture was founded by Bill Mollison and David Holmgren in 1978 and was inspired by the sheer complexity and fruitfulness of the natural world. Permaculturalists recognise the need to work in synergy with living systems, understanding how one part of nature fulfils the needs of another, and to consciously design our own inter-ventions so as to work with, and not against, natural proc-esses. When faced with an agricultural task a conventional farmer would think big scale, plough it up, put on fertiliser, spray against pests, harvest etc. In contrast a permaculturist is likely first to stop and learn what nature is already doing in the particular type of soil and through the different micro-climates that are present. Then they would design what they planned to grow so as to fit in with the natural systems that are there and minimise interventions and energy use. The fascinating thing about permaculture is that once you start to think in this way the vision expands so that these principles become a vision for a different kind of human life. The per-maculturists naturally make a bridge between how we treat the earth and how we treat each other. They spontaneously value and celebrate human community and have even come to appreciate faith. David Holmgren himself was brought up as an atheist, but says that 'through the project of permaculture, my life is by small increments being drawn towards some kind of spiritual awareness and perspective that is not yet clear[97].'Living the dream is clearly a powerful stimulus to faith.

# Trust

Travel is certain to become more precious in the future and that will mean a revival of neighbourhood. The transition away from fossil fuels is going to present enormous issues for electricity generation, but the issues around travel are likely to be even more formidable. People will simply find more of life closer to home. Although we may rail against the lack of choice that accompanies transport restrictions we will enjoy a stronger system of relationships, extended families may recover their vitality as family members choose to live closer to each other and all of our social networks may grow stronger and more meaningful. We need to build local neighbourhood ready for the future.

One grassroots organisation that seems to be calling people back to something authentically human is the Transition Network. This owes its origins to Rob Hopkins, who has inspired groups around the country with the idea that we should make a deliberate plan to change the way that we are living so as to 'transition' to a new kind of life, moving away from our dependency on oil and relearning a whole set of skills to do with growing food, reusing goods, and renewing local neighbourhoods. One set of people who know something about living like this are those who lived during the Second World War. Sarah Pugh in Bristol has set up a small group

...............................................

97　　　David Holmgren *Permaculture – principles and pathways beyond sustainability* 2002 Holmgren Design Services page 3 called 'Older women for the planet' which is about some of our older people sharing their insights about how to make do and mend, how to grow and cook food, and barter in times of necessity. It sounds like a great way to honour our elders and recognise their ongoing contribution to our communities. David Attenborough is on record as saying that we need just such a wartime cooperative spirit if we are to face the challenges of climate change.

Another idea we have been exploring in Bristol is to work with ancestry in relation to local communities and people. I have been impressed as to how powerful it can be to help someone research their roots. It is like you are helping them fill in the story that this modern consumerist society has taken away and it seems to minister to the soul at some deep level. We have developed a multi-faceted project called *The Tree of Life* on an outer estate in Bristol called Knowle West. One aspect of it is to help people discover their origins, affirm them as people and build the local stories. It feels like a worthwhile thing to do and it naturally seems to combine with the other concerns of *The Tree of Life* namely the environment, social justice and the creative arts.

I believe that this revival of neighbourhood will be an enormous blessing to us, strengthening and extending the face to face relational networks that we all have, giving our lives new purpose and direction and contributing markedly to human happiness. In the face of all the dire predictions of the future this bit is truly good news. We may actually end up living far more satisfying lives than we do now.

Of course there are dangers too. As people try to break free of the shackles of our present culture, they will naturally want to experiment with new ways of living. Some will fall into the trap of thinking that human community can be anything that we want it to be. They will then try to set up their utopia and be terribly hurt when it fails. History teaches us that such idealism perennially rears its head at times of radical change. It needs to. Some people must press the boundaries, especially at moments like this, but we would be fools if we did not heed the serious lessons from human history about the way that people tend to behave in groups, their potential for oppression, how naivety can produce abhorrent power structures[98] or how anarchy can lead to paralysis of decision making[99]. I have some friends who, like me, were caught up in Christian community experiments in the seventies. Sometimes I will ask them about these times. Most of them stare at their boots and go quiet at this point. It is too painful to talk about.

We need wisdom about human behaviour, but we must not be put off. The relational life of people in the developed world is often very weak indeed. Anxieties springing from loneliness are commonplace. And the potential reinvigoration of neighbourhood and community in response to the environmental challenge is an enormous opportunity.

# Celebration

We have dramatically undervalued celebration. People need to gather and play. In so doing we form powerful social bonds and affirm what we understand to be good among us. Before the Reformation every community in this country had a whole set of annual celebrations, many of a religious character, which were kept by communities and which felt like great fun to everyone, even those who had no particular faith.

..............................................

98     As illustrated by an almost endless litany of cultish groups through history.

99     For example, Carolyn Steel in Hungry City notes how Robert Owen's 'New Harmony' community in Indiana spent two years bickering over how to run the community and finally ran out of cash.

Since that time the number of public holidays has declined significantly and people's interest in local carnivals and festivals has waned. We prefer now to be entertained by the TV and some rarely go out to meet their neighbours, let alone celebrate with them.

To some extent the local festival has been displaced by the gigantic gathering, the Glastonbury or the City-wide event. I think gigantic gatherings have a place and EarthAbbey will have an annual Earth Camp through which we hope to consolidate the movement, give people a sense of belonging and celebrate what has been achieved. Yet I think we also should take advantage of the revival of neighbourhood by reinventing local celebrations. As green community groups form in neighbourhoods across the world, let's take the opportunity to reinvent carnival, have an annual shindig where people let their hair down with dancing, live music, feasting and the like. It will be fun. It will also build the movement. And it is part of the dream.

Also at a more personal level, why not set aside one day each year to celebrate the earth with your friends? In EarthAbbey we are calling this an Earth Day, as an extra to birthday. It is just another excuse to celebrate really and use the celebration to be with friends and play.

In a culture dominated by key performance indicators, much of the energy and creativity of people has drained away. Celebration can be one way of nurturing creative talent. It can also be associated with a revival of the creative arts and the development of new craft skills. Arts trails are an obvious example of this already happening. I also expect to see ancient crafts rediscovered, adapted and shown off through celebration as we search for a more earth-friendly way of living.

# Peace

Peace is easy to say and difficult to do. Jesus' life would suggest that peace needs to be made, not simply found. Lifestyle can achieve a great deal, transforming our inner lives, binding us into powerful communities and providing practical models for future life, yet there will remain a vital place for campaigning. In biblical terms campaigning is a prophetic activity. It is designed to provoke the conscience, particularly of those in authority and open up the ground for genuine and truthful negotiation. We think of Jeremiah, Isaiah, Amos and Jesus himself, and consider those who have gone before us, daring to speak and act radically in the world, confront the authorities, even risk their own lives, for the sake of speaking the truth as they saw it from God. These people opened up the world of their day. We need those who will do the same for us.

The whole idea of political action makes some people uneasy. Perhaps that is in part because we have domesticated Jesus. I don't know what it was, maybe it was all that time in the wilderness, but Jesus had a wild side. In fact this is part of his attractiveness to some. The story of Jesus turning over the tables in the temple causes an intake of breath among the tame. 'Oh dear' gentle Jesus meek and mild has just broken his cover. Something real, something slightly dangerous has just emerged.

Wildness may be an underrated virtue. Religions commonly cultivate tame people. A tame person is careful not to offend, fits in with cultural norms and is 'nice' and gentle. Yet creative challenge necessitates a degree of wildness. Wild people are an endangered species in the church. For years they have been subtly excluded, made to feel uncomfortable, gently driven out. The person in touch with their wildness will dare to speak the truth without concern for the consequence. They are an exciting and dangerous person to be with. It is through the wild person that others sense hope. They are mould breakers. They challenge oppressive institutions. They confront people and issues that others shy away from. And they have a tendency to suffer for it. It is a mistake to think that authentic Christianity is nice.

It was about a year ago that I came home from a holiday and said to my wife, 'I have to make a polar bear'. It is an elaborate construction, really big, with stilts for the front legs and a head shaped out of chicken wire and fibre glass attached to a bike helmet. To be in the polar bear is a strange experience. You are like in a different world. I have found myself praying there and trying to imagine the condition that polar bears find themselves in today. From outside it is also rather mysterious. People can't quite work out how the human fits in it. 'Are there two people', say some of the children? Or 'Is it animatronic?', they ask as I lumber about with my minder, advertising some environmental event or campaign. As polar bear I have been kicked, patted and even groped, but have generally been amazed at the positive response that it creates. People immediately know what it is about. My minder hardly has to say the words 'Climate Change' at all, while people respond with 'Good on you for doing it'. For my part, I am pleased that the polar bear evokes compassion, though I have become a little hesitant about this misrepresenting of an amazing creature. It may be all too easy to see the polar bear as soft and cuddly, when it is truly a magnificent and fearsome beast.

That's enough about the polar bear. I guess I wanted to tell that story to encourage us to do the unusual. The possibilities are endless. Have you ever thought of clowning for example? Jo Wilding pioneered an extraordinarily brave way of using clowns in Iraq in the service of peacemaking.[100] Clowns and court jesters have proved their value in history as bearers of grief and purveyors of shocking truth.

In recent years the summer holiday period has been marked by something called Climate Camp. For those who have been there it has often been a life changing experience. Many young people tell of it as a moment of commitment to the environmental challenge. Some of their stories sound almost like the testimonies that you hear in churches. It is also a moment of challenge to the society. In 2007 it was a challenge to the building of the new runway at Heathrow airport. In 2008 they confronted the redevelopment of Kingsnorth coal-fuelled power station. Careful choice of target, wise actions that challenge, but do not alienate the watching public, awakening consciences to gospel imperatives, this is the stuff of prophetic work. We need it and we need more of it, if we are to respond in time. As we saw in Chapter six our call today can be understood in terms of the three elements – 'repent', then 'live' and 'proclaim' the gospel of peace for all creation. Proclaiming and campaigning are twin sisters. We cannot do without campaigning.

So there we have a few ideas relating to the six themes that express this great biblical dream of the world-as-it-should-be. They are no more than that, because I believe that you and I need to express these things in a whole host of ways and no centrally constructed set of programmes can do justice to the creative ingenuity that is in you. I invite you to treat each of these themes as like a bowl into which you can pour your own ingredients and cook up your own delicious meal.

........................................

100    See Jo Wilding *Dont shoot the clowns* New Internationalist 2006

# Endpiece

If you have come this far, the thing I would most like to encourage you to do is to simply embark on this journey. It is a journey to a whole new kind of life. None of us quite knows the detail of what we will meet along the way, but I am clear that we have to set out. Rather like the patriarch Abraham, we have to set out, 'not knowing what lies before us'. I am only clear that we have to live more in tune with the earth and that we need to walk together. In a sense each of us starts from a different place. Each of us may have different priorities, but we need to walk. Every step on the journey will mean that we see the world as from a new place, going deeper into a truer and more worthwhile sort of existence. We must beware of all finger wagging. Never has Jesus' parable of the two people who went up to the temple to pray been more pertinent. We cannot afford to be Pharisees who thank God that they 'do this and do that' and 'not like that other person over there'. Instead we must begin with a deep awareness of our shortcomings. Surely none of us is squeaky clean in our oil-addicted society? So let us have mercy on each other as we walk this path, careful not to condemn or look sideways at the naive person who comes among us. But let's be content to walk the road, together, to find the new way of life that God is calling us to.

One of the questions that we may want to take on this journey is one about our uniqueness. I wonder, have you seriously engaged with the idea that you have a unique calling in life that *only* you can fulfil? Are you currently trapped into a life that is just turning the handle, conformed to the dominant culture around you and unable to break free? After reading this book you may recognise that there is something that God is calling you to do. It may be something that only you can do, in this moment, in your situation? It may sound altogether too grand to say this, but maybe the earth is waiting for you to respond? Maybe God is waiting for you to respond? As we have seen, the apostle Paul was clear that the work of Christ applied to the whole creation. He looked forward to the renewal of the whole creation as the heart of the Christian hope and he said that 'Creation waits for the revealing of the children of God'. Perhaps now is the moment of our revealing. Many have said that this generation will decide the future of the planet. Will you rise up and live the life you are being called to - with all the energy that God inspires? The coming generations may come to thank us if we do.

# Postscript
# Three resources to help you on your journey

EarthAbbey is producing a course entitled **"A Journey to a New Kind of Life"**. It is designed for small groups of between 4 and 12 people and takes a spiritual look at behaviour change. It begins from our own personal stories and each week engages with a different aspect of life, taking us through the resources of the earth, the natural world, money, travel, holidays, neighbours etc and inviting participants to take a step toward a more earth-friendly life. Resources include the sort of biblical engagement that is in this book. Some have described it as a cross between Alcoholics Anonymous and a Methodist Class as it helps us face our addiction and confront necessary behavioural change! You may find that "A Journey to a New Kind of Life" is a way that you can get together with others to explore the ideas in this book.

We also have available a meditative trail known as **"Earth Connect"**

**Earth Connect** is an interactive trail created by Janet Lunt and Chris Sunderland in the style of a labyrinth with ten 'stations' or stopping places along its route where people are encouraged to experience and reflect on some aspect of the natural world.

The trail is built around a highly accessible, 'light touch' Christian spirituality, which is designed to encourage a broad range of people to explore their own thoughts and feelings about our relationship with the natural world

It is designed for a large building like a church or hall. It can also be used in schools where individual stations can form part of an RE or Citizenship lesson

The **Earth Connect** pack consists of a series of laminated cards describing how to set up each station plus a CD containing graphics that can be printed out and mounted onto boards. Setting up the trail is an artistic project and will require someone with an interest in style and form.

Or finally, If you are interested in encouraging your local community into action on an environmental agenda then you might like to consider using our **EarthWorks** café-style conversation. This is designed to create an open space where a diverse group of people can share their own stories and explore their unique callings and energies in this area so as to produce an effective local environmental group.

**All these resources are available through the Earth Abbey website www.earthabbey.com**